PURPOSE

&

PASSION

COMPILED BY
PEACE MITCHELL &
KATY GARNER

WOMEN CHANGING THE WORLD PRESS

Women Changing the World Press acknowledges the Elders and Traditional owners of country throughout Australia and their connection to lands, waters and communities. We pay our respect to Elders past and present and extend that respect to all Aboriginal and Islander peoples today. We honour more than sixty thousand years of Indigenous women's voices, stories, leadership and wisdom.

Edited by Tracy Regan

Typeset in Adobe Garamond Pro 12/17pt

A catalogue record for this work is available from the National Library of Australia

National Library of Australia Catalogue-in-Publication data:
Purpose & Passion/Peace Mitchell and Katy Garner

ISBN:
9781763658240
(Paperback)

For those who feel called for greatness. May you always have the courage to follow your purpose and passion.

Contents

Let the Past Empower Your Future

Alexie Better

DEDICATION

I dedicate this chapter to my parents, husband and son, expressing my deepest gratitude for your unwavering love, kindness and support. Your presence in my life fuels my determination, reminding me I am never alone on this journey. My love for each of you knows no bounds.

Additionally, I extend heartfelt thanks to my grade four teacher. Your perseverance and dedication never faltered, and your impact on my life remains profound. The lessons you imparted years ago have inspired me to assist others facing learning obstacles.

MY STORY

My journey doesn't begin in the present moment; it traces back to my primary school days. I recall feeling adrift amidst a crowd of classmates, struggling with the complexities of learning and grappling with questions for which I lacked answers. School posed a constant challenge for me, and life itself often felt terribly overwhelming.

One particular day stands out vividly in my memory, marking a pivotal moment that would alter the path of my life forever. It was during a creative writing session, when our assignment was to create an imaginative piece. Writing had always been a struggle for me; spelling seemed an insurmountable hurdle, and summoning the courage to read aloud required an extraordinary effort. Typically, I would simply improvise on the spot, pretending I had composed the piece beforehand.

On that significant day, I found myself fighting with a seemingly simple word: 'key'. A single syllable, three letters long, yet it eluded me entirely. Each student had the option to consult the teacher for spelling assistance by referencing our 'Word Bank Book'. Mine was nearly filled to capacity. Summoning my courage, I approached the teacher and inquired about its spelling. Her reaction pierced me to the core, her expression flat, eyes rolling, shoulders slumping, as she uttered with palpable disdain, 'Not again.' My heart ached, tears welling in my eyes, as I retreated to my desk desperate to evade notice.

What this teacher failed to realise was that I was dyslexic. Dyslexia is when an individual processes information differently. Letters can flip around and it can be difficult to remember words or phrases. It can be challenging to even understand conversations if words are spoken too fast.

My journey was fraught with obstacles as I navigated through school. Tutor after tutor, lesson after lesson, I gradually found reading, writing and learning less difficult. Throughout my schooling, the question lingered in my mind: *What do I want to pursue?* Thankfully, my persistence, along with the unwavering belief of my supportive parents, was instrumental in helping me overcome numerous challenges.

At eighteen, my mother, a psychologist, suggested I work with autistic children as the demand for aides was high. This sparked my journey of assisting struggling children, particularly those with neurodiversity and learning difficulties. Reflecting on my upbringing, I was driven to prevent others from enduring similar struggles and feelings of being unsupported.

Fast-forward to today, I am now the proud owner of Better Multisensory Learning Centre, a specialised educational clinic. With my surname embedded in the business name, I offer support to children with autism, dyslexia, ADHD, speech delays, intellectual disabilities and other developmental disorders. Our services encompass developmental education, counselling, parent support and coaching, school assistance and diagnostic assessments for learning, as well as providing psychological assistance to help students of all ages with their emotional and psychological wellbeing. I am grateful for the opportunity to pursue my passion and collaborate with exceptional individuals.

My clinic holds profound significance for me; it is a sanctuary where I support individuals across all age groups. Families embarking on journeys akin to my own find solace here, receiving the same support I once did as a teenager with learning difficulties. Despite the challenges inherent on this journey, it is one of patience, compassion and unwavering dedication for all those who receive our services.

In dedicating this chapter, I extend my heartfelt appreciation to those who have faced neurodiversity and learning challenges, encouraging them to embark on their own path towards establishing a learning centre or launching their own business.

LESSONS IN RUNNING A BUSINESS

Over the past seven years, I have accumulated a wealth of lessons in areas like business management, client relations, staffing and operational procedures. Yet, foundational to any business endeavour is establishing clear goals and a strong business model.

FOR ME

Goal: My aim was to support neurodiverse individuals, including those with dyslexia, autism spectrum, ADHD, speech and language delays, intellectual disabilities and various other learning challenges and developmental disorders.

Business model: I envisioned offering specialised interventions such as educational support (in literacy and numeracy), therapy, counselling and diagnostic assessments tailored to the needs of neurodiverse and learning-challenged individuals.

The key question then arose: How would this business model and structure operate? My solution involved collaborating with speech pathologists, psychologists and other allied professionals already engaged in assisting neurodiverse individuals. This collaborative approach ensured a comprehensive and holistic support system for our clients.

EXPERIENCE

Before venturing into entrepreneurship, I recognised the need for hands-on practical experience beyond what high school and university could offer.

During my university years, and in the time following graduation, I seized the opportunity to work at a psychology clinic specialising in assessments, therapy and support for neurodiverse individuals. Beginning as a receptionist, I managed client administration, gradually expanding my skills by training as an ABA (applied behaviour analysis) therapist, while still at university. The clinic afforded me the chance to provide therapy to children on the autism spectrum. As I progressed, I also pursued a teaching certification and integrated my teaching skills with ABA therapy to offer developmental education support to children within the autism spectrum.

Working in the psychology clinic provided invaluable life and business lessons, bridging the gaps left by my learning difficulties. Through hands-on experience:

- I learned to apply theoretical knowledge in real-world scenarios, strengthening my understanding through communication, problem-solving and decision-making situations.
- Despite inevitable setbacks and failures, I discovered they catalysed innovation and creativity, prompting me to seek guidance from diverse mentors to refine my communication skills, intervention approach and program systems approaches.
- Armed with years of experience and new-found knowledge, I embarked on the journey of establishing my own independent clinic, Better Multisensory Learning.

This new venture was daunting, particularly given my learning challenges. However, fuelled by support, research and unwavering determination, I remained committed to realising my dream. Thus, I forged ahead, ready to put into practice everything I'd learned and experienced along the way.

LOCATION

Selecting the right location for your business is paramount, as it can significantly impact its success. Several factors should be considered:

1. **Visibility and accessibility:** An optimal location ensures your business is easily noticeable and accessible to potential clients. Premises tucked away may not attract passing traffic. Co-locating with complementary services can also enhance visibility. In my case, although there are other tutoring centres nearby, each caters to different needs, as ours focuses on neurodiversity.

2. **Target market:** Proximity to your target clientele enhances the likelihood of attracting and retaining customers. I strategically positioned my centre near several schools, on a busy thoroughfare within a strip shopping centre with steady foot traffic. Additionally, an outdoor poster board grabs the attention of passersby, further increasing visibility and accessibility.

3. **Future growth potential:** Opt for a location that facilitates future expansion and adapting to new opportunities. After three years, I found it necessary to consider either securing additional office space or relocating closer to other specialists aiding neurodiverse individuals, aligning with the evolving needs of my organisation.

Ultimately, selecting the right location lays the groundwork for the long-term success and sustainability of your business.

MARKETING

Developing a robust marketing strategy is essential for attracting customers. Here are the steps and strategies that proved effective for me:

1. **Identify the target audience:** Understand the demographics and educational needs of students. In my case, I focused on individuals with neurodiversity.

2. **Create a unique selling proposition:** Highlight what sets your business apart from the competition. Emphasise your unique services, creative techniques and exceptional facilities. I showcased the experienced educators, counsellors and psychologists on my team, along with the evidence-based approaches tailored to assist individuals with learning needs.

3. **Build a professional website:** Your website is your online representation. Ensure it has a unique domain, user-friendly design, easy

access to information and is optimised for search engines. My website provides detailed information about our services, the types of neurodiversity and learning challenges we support, as well as staff profiles. This has become a primary source of new enquiries.

4. **Utilise content marketing:** Create informative blog posts, articles and videos for your audience. Share this content on social media platforms like Facebook, Instagram and LinkedIn. I regularly post on Facebook about our centre and the services we offer, resulting in a substantial following and consistent referral source.

5. **Collaborate with local communities and organisations:** Increase your reach and reputation by partnering with local groups and participating in community events. Sponsorships and professional outreach demonstrate your dedication. I've donated time via professional development sessions to local schools and engaged with experts in the community, leading to several schools referring clients to our centre.

By implementing strategies and continuously refining your approach, you can effectively market your business and attract clients who align with your services.

POLICIES AND PROCEDURES

Establishing clear policies and procedures is essential for the smooth operation and integrity of any new business. Here are some key areas to address:

1. **New client enrolment:** Define a procedure for enrolling new clients, outlining the required documentation and information necessary before services can be provided.

2. **Service delivery:** Detail how services will be delivered to ensure consistency and quality for all clients.

3. **Safety policies:** Develop safety policies covering emergency procedures, health protocols and facility upkeep to safeguard the wellbeing of students, staff and visitors.

4. **Intake process:** Describe how client information is obtained, handled and protected in compliance with relevant laws and regulations. For instance, at my clinic, we collaborated with a psychologist to develop a comprehensive client history questionnaire and consent form.

5. **Complaint handling:** Establish processes for clients and staff to report and resolve concerns. Despite best efforts, customer complaints may arise, and having clear procedures in place ensures timely and effective resolution.

6. **Regular review and update:** Continuously review and update policies and procedures to align with the evolving needs of the business and to remain compliant with legal requirements and industry standards.

Overall, organising policies and procedures protects your business and enhances its professionalism. Consulting with legal professionals or industry experts can ensure your documentation meets regulatory standards.

HIRING STAFF

Hiring staff is a crucial step in the growth and success of any business. Here are some key considerations to keep in mind:

1. **Define the job description:** Clearly outline the responsibilities, qualifications and skills required for the position, as well as its importance within the organisation. In my case, I prioritised hiring individuals with expertise in learning difficulties and counselling, to align with the needs of my business.

2. **Integration process:** Develop a comprehensive onboarding process to help new staff assimilate smoothly into the organisation. Provide them with training, resources and ongoing support to ensure their success in their new role. In my experience, I offer weekly mentoring sessions, quarterly training sessions and access to a range of resources to support their professional development.

3. **Follow-up and support:** Regularly check in with new staff, addressing any concerns or questions they may have. Open communication and support are essential for fostering a positive work environment and ensuring employee satisfaction.

While hiring new staff can be challenging, it's important to trust your instincts, maintain transparency and be responsive to the needs of your employees. By prioritising their success and wellbeing, you can cultivate a dedicated and motivated team that contributes to the growth and success of your business.

ENGAGING WITH ENQUIRIES AND CLIENTS

Engaging with enquiries and clients is crucial for nurturing positive relationships and fostering trust. Here are several effective strategies:

1. **Prompt response:** Prioritise timely responses to enquiries and clients. Aim to address emails, calls and messages within twenty-four hours to demonstrate professionalism and dedication to customer service.

2. **Personalisation:** Tailor your communication to meet the unique needs and preferences of each client. Offer personalised solutions or advice whenever possible, drawing on your understanding of various needs to provide relevant support.

3. **Provide valuable information:** Offer useful resources to address client enquiries and concerns. Share articles, case studies and information

about your services to empower clients to make informed decisions.

4. **Follow-up:** Follow up with clients after initial enquiries to ensure their needs are met and to maintain satisfaction. Consistent follow-up can also encourage repeat business and referrals, further strengthening client relationships.

5. **Offer multiple communication channels:** Provide clients with various communication options such as phone, email, social media and in-person consultations. Accommodating clients' preferred communication methods enhances accessibility and convenience.

By implementing these strategies, you can effectively engage with enquiries and clients, fostering positive relationships and ultimately contributing to business success.

BUILDING A CONTACT DATABASE

Building a comprehensive contact database is essential for networking and fostering professional connections, especially in fields like education. Here are some tips to help you build and maintain a solid database:

1. **Start early:** Begin identifying and collecting contact information of individuals affiliated with your profession or business as soon as possible. Over time, this will enable you to develop a substantial database of contacts.

2. **Research and identify:** Conduct research to identify key individuals, organisations and institutions relevant to your field. In my case, it included educators, therapists, professionals and educational institutions.

3. **Networking events:** Attend networking events, conferences and workshops related to your industry to meet new contacts and expand your network. Be proactive in exchanging contact information and following up with potential connections.

4. **Use online platforms:** Leverage online platforms, such as LinkedIn, to connect with professionals in your field and expand your network. Join relevant groups and participate in discussions to engage with others in your industry.

5. **Stay organised:** Maintain a well-organised database using software or tools designed for contact management. Keep detailed records of contact information, interactions and any relevant notes to facilitate effective communication and follow-up.

HERE ARE SOME ADDITIONAL TIPS FOR MANAGING LEARNING CHALLENGES WHILE RUNNING A BUSINESS

1. **Templates:** Create email templates to streamline communication and save time. This eliminates the need to rewrite information and ensures consistency in your messaging.

2. **Reviewing:** Seek assistance from trusted individuals, such as family members, friends or professional peers, to review important documents and provide feedback. A fresh perspective can help identify errors or areas for improvement.

3. **Utilise online resources:** Take advantage of online tools and resources designed to support individuals with learning challenges. This may include immersive readers, browser extensions for modifying text formatting and other accessibility features which enhance reading and writing capabilities.

By implementing these strategies and utilising available resources, you can effectively build and maintain a contact database while managing learning challenges in your business endeavours. Remember to stay positive, seek support when needed and continue learning and growing in your journey.

RECOMMENDATIONS

Certainly, amidst the hustle and bustle of entrepreneurship, it is crucial to prioritise balance between work and personal life. As a wife, mother, daughter, sister and friend, nurturing these relationships and taking care of your mental and physical health is paramount. Remember to carve out time for relaxation, reflection and self-celebration, acknowledging your achievements and allowing yourself to recharge.

I hope this chapter has provided you with valuable insights, dos and don'ts, and most importantly, courage. Courage to pursue your dreams, to embrace your uniqueness and to navigate your journey with confidence. Always remember you are not alone. Regardless of your neurodiversity, your journey is yours to own, and it is bound to be extraordinary. Keep moving forward, keep dreaming big and keep believing in yourself!

Alexie Better

B.S.Sc, Master of Teaching
INPP cert, ABA cert Adolescent Counselling cert
Developmental Educator & Specialist in Dyslexia Education
Director, Better Multisensory Learning Centre

Alexie Better is a committed developmental educator and literacy specialist driven by a dedication to nurturing learning. With a background in teaching and counselling, Alexie has over fourteen years of experience as a specialist literacy tutor and developmental educator. Her approach is characterised by a distinctive perspective, aiming to cultivate inclusive and captivating learning environments conducive to the flourishing of all students in primary and secondary schools.

Alexie has refined her expertise in developmental education, prioritising a deep understanding of each learner's individual needs and implementing tailored strategies to facilitate their academic and personal growth and progress. Whether assisting students with learning disabilities and dyslexia, language barriers, ADHD, autism spectrum or other developmental obstacles, Alexie approaches each person with patience, empathy and an unwavering commitment to finding effective solutions that cater to their unique circumstances.

In her role as a developmental educator, Alexie champions literacy and numeracy as essential tools for empowerment and achievement. She tirelessly endeavours to ignite a love for reading and writing in her students, equipping them with the skills and confidence necessary to navigate the complexities of the academic world with ease.

Alexie is recognised for her compassionate teaching approach and her ability to forge meaningful connections with her students. She firmly believes in the transformative power of education to shape lives and is dedicated to making a positive impact in the lives of her students, empowering them to realise their full potential and embrace a lifelong journey of learning.

Don't Fear the Dark

All the Light You Need Is Within You

Amy Hall

For Damien, who gifted me unconditional love and acceptance.
For Jack and Grace, who gave me my purpose.

When I was a young girl, I was acutely aware of my *difference*. My personality was colourful, curious, always challenging and questioning life around me, but I was told to blend in. My sense of self-advocacy and independence was described as strong and loud, which was intimidating to others and challenged the ingrained view of people around me. They simply didn't know what to make of me.

To make life easier, they tried to bring me back into line with what they felt I needed to be, as if it was for my own good. People who looked, behaved or, in fact, *were* noticeably unique were an easy target. I was encouraged to dress, speak and behave in a way that matched what was expected and, inevitably, what was perceived as safe. I was taught to 'mask' who I was, but all this did was confuse me and set me on a track of authentic self-discovery that continues to this day.

LESSON 1 – KNOW WHO YOU ARE AND DO IT ON PURPOSE

I never felt like I fit in with my peers. I felt awkward and didn't understand how other people thought about the same things I did. I walked through most of my childhood with only a small handful of friends and I now understand I was sublimely out of my depth. I was trying to behave aligned with others but, but even when I did, was often not rewarded with the connections I so deeply craved.

School was a place I dreaded. I was constantly bullied and beaten by students multiple times, for reasons I didn't understand. Even just the way I waved to say hello to other students caused reactions. In one year, I sustained three nasty head injuries; all of this before my thirteenth birthday. What followed these attacks were years of neurological problems that I now believe caused a lasting brain injury, impacting my memory and the way I learn. It also infused a fear into my bones I've never been able to shake off completely. Experts call this trauma.

My teen years were challenging, but by my sixteenth birthday, I started the process of learning who I was, what I believed and how I wanted to behave and communicate. I didn't know it at the time, but I was finally learning that being who I was, was not a bad thing and I didn't need to mask or hide who I was.

I was reading poetry that taught me about relationships. The melodrama of so many Shakespearean couples matched the depth of feeling I had for those I loved. I realised what I was feeling was okay, because it was played out in those famous and grand love stories. I was watching the same movies repeatedly and knew the dialogue of so many of them; they helped me form social scripts, finding ways to communicate what I wanted to say when I couldn't put the words together myself. I would play make-believe for hours with my toys, long after an age where one would normally put such items away. I would create long elaborate stories and act them out in a way that would help me understand the scenarios I was observing in others.

These early experiences shaped my identity. I now know I was a not a strange or awkward creature who couldn't rely on or trust her own thoughts and feelings, but a beautifully imperfect neurodivergent misunderstood little girl, building the foundations of a strong, courageous, adaptive and resilient woman.

Part of this process of accepting and authentically owning my identity, with all its imperfections, quirks and evolutions, has been through challenging the expectations of others. I've always been a deeply passionate person, but this passion was never celebrated. One of the enduring themes of childhood, especially at school, was the emphasis that being wrong, making mistakes or being non-compliant would come with grave consequences, including rejection. This followed me into adulthood, carrying with me a great weight of anxiety and the dreaded imposter syndrome. Despite my best efforts in any task or endeavour, my own inner voice whispered, *Not good enough, do better, be better.* As an adult, I was still expected to mask my passion and my quirkiness, especially in the workplace, as this was referred to as exuberance and often didn't fit well with my colleagues. Words like *neurotic, quirky, strange, highly strung* and *odd* were frequently applied to me. Ironically, the students I taught, the clients I gravitated to and those I supported in my career described my work ethic as refreshing, different, motivating and inspiring. So, who was correct? I had learned to listen to the views and opinions of others to elucidate the truth, and I wasn't encouraged to listen to my instinct or trust my own reasoning.

Now, I surround myself with exceptional teachers, mentors and safe people. They have taught me that who I am is an offering for good to the world, not something to be intimidated by. I often ask for guidance, and while my brain still must contend with fear of being wrong, these safe people now reinforce that I know the answers to most of the questions or worries I have. I know the next steps, and even if I'm wrong, I know I can endure and learn from these experiences. Being wrong does not equate to failure, rather a necessary step in my growth. With an unconditional self-acceptance, I have learned to trust myself and believe I am worth knowing. Most importantly, I have learned to know who I am and *do it on purpose.*

LESSON 2 – IF THEY DON'T GIVE YOU A PLACE AT THE TABLE, DRAG ACROSS A FOLDING CHAIR

Something I always knew growing up was that I wanted to be of service to others.

The seeds were planted when I was about seven years old. I had run away from home after an argument with my mother and packed my belongings into a backpack, mainly containing my toys and a very large teddy bear. I was a willful child and I walked, alone, 500m down the road towards my beloved Nanny's home to seek refuge. But I struggled with the weight of my backpack, and as people walked by me, I can remember thinking, *Can't they see I need help? Why is no-one helping me?* From that moment, I knew I wanted to help others. I knew that service would be a feature to my purpose.

At school, I was the person who sought to play with the lonely children. I would give away my lunch or my jumper when a friend needed it, and I attracted friends who were struggling or seeking to ease their pain in some way. Doing these things for others made up for what I desperately wanted someone to do for me, so it eased my own pain as well.

I became a school teacher, but I was conflicted. I felt that measuring achievements by testing and scrutinising children based on a set of arbitrary measures were misaligned to my own values. This was especially true of our support of students and children with disabilities. At that point in my career, I hadn't fully accepted my own disability identity, but I was acutely aware of the impact that deficit-based practices could have on a child's delicate and evolving identity. For around ten years, I did what I felt I was supposed to do, in a way that was accepted. I'm reminded of a beautiful quote from the 1998 film, *Patch Adams*: 'I've had several jobs, moved several places, nothing seemed to fit, I don't seem to fit.' This summarised my experience in my early career. But rather than sit in this internal conflict, I listened to the incredible Maya Angelou's wisdom, 'If you don't like something, change it. If you can't change it, change your attitude. Don't complain.'

So, I made a change and became a behaviour support practitioner, specialising in helping children with disabilities, which ultimately led to me starting my own business providing a range of support services assisting families to help their children grow and develop. My preferred clientele were children who presented with multiple complex challenges and their families who were living under extreme stress and pressure trying to maintain quality of life. This became my passion and I feel so privileged that this is my vocation.

As has been the resounding truth across my life, every experience leads you to what you are meant to learn. My journey has led me to learn from incredible people, and their legacy in my story has been to impart valuable lessons and accumulated knowledge I can share with others.

My favourite *Grey's Anatomy* quote is, 'Sometimes the future changes quickly and completely and we're left with the choice of what to do next. We can choose to be afraid of it, to stand there trembling and not moving, assuming the worst, or we can step forward into the unknown and assume it will be brilliant.'

I never thought I would start a business, let alone be called a leader in my field. But this has been where my journey has landed. I stopped wondering why I wasn't given a place at the table and decided to drag across a chair and claim a place for myself.

LESSON 3 – BE A BLANKET IN SOMEONE'S SNOWSTORM

In 2020, in the middle of the COVID-19 pandemic, in Sydney and away from my regional community, I gave birth to my daughter, who was fourteen weeks premature. To say this was a challenge is an understatement, in regard to both her birth and what followed.

I had been living in hospital for several weeks prior to her birth, trying desperately to keep her snug within me. Alas, all the medicine in the world couldn't keep my very strong and determined daughter from entering the world. When she was born, I silently prayed she would stay alive, and that whatever came from having such an underdeveloped little body and brain, I would have the strength to carry her through whatever disability, barrier or struggle she may face. I was separated from my other child; at home with family, the worldwide pandemic affecting us all and preventing me from spending time with her father in hospital. I only saw her in his arms when she was nine weeks old; the day she had her first bath. Honestly, the trauma of this experience pushed my sanity to the edge many times.

At around four weeks old, I was able to nurse her on my chest, despite her being attached to the multiple tubes, wires and oxygen apparatus keeping her alive. I was only able to hold her for around three hours a day, before her little body would say, *I'm done now, put me back in my bed and let me grow.* I look back now and think how torturous it felt to put her back, watching her inside her plastic incubator for the rest of the day.

But on this particular day, right after I had placed her back to sleep, I checked my emails and saw a message from my employer informing me my desk had been packed up and my clients told I was not coming back to work, as I was now on maternity leave. My manager wished me well, but it crushed me. I had worked hard in my role as a behaviour and early intervention specialist for children with disabilities and was eager to meet the expectations of my bosses, whom I respected deeply.

Talk about timing. I was away from home, isolated from my family, with no support network and very few people to share this very scary experience with. My community at work was now gone and the thought of my desk being packed up reinforced a feeling that I was just another cog in the wheel; very replaceable and somewhat insignificant.

My business was born in that moment. I thought to myself, *This is not the way you lead. I can do better than this. I can be the captain of my own ship and steer a course that can make a difference for clients and families. How hard can it be to start my own business?* My next thought was to wonder what my point of difference could be. What could I offer differently in my business, in the way of knowledge, support, service and empowering families living with disabilities? I had expertise, knowledge, a commitment to excellence and an unreservedly open mind to learning *from them* how I might meet their service expectations.

I never wanted to feel insignificant in my workplace again. I wanted to take back power in my career. I knew if I gave myself half a chance, I would be able to make a strong meaningful difference to the lives of those who wanted to work with me.

Since my business began in 2021, I have supported over three hundred families across Australia. I have led a team of clinicians to support rural and regional communities who lack access to good support systems. I have developed and released a national training program to support the induction and training of behaviour practitioners, so they can better support, empower and understand the needs of children and young people with a complex disability, and their needs. I am a mentor to over forty practitioners, nationally, to guide and support their work with others. I am recognised as a business leader in my community, having won multiple business and disability leadership awards, both nationally and internationally.

This was the origin of my business, and I am finally living an authentic life, both personally and professionally. My passion has a home. My purpose is clear.

I'm proud to make my living doing work that is aligned with my values, and I know that even when I get it wrong, as we all inevitably do, I still leave the world better than I found it.

From a little girl who was beaten because she was different and whose unique and gentle disposition unnerved others who didn't understand her, to a scared teenager, desperately uncertain about who she was and her place in the world, to a mother of two beautiful neurodivergent children, I finally feel I have reached a point where I know who I am. This empowers me to encourage others to stand in their own power; to embrace all the beautiful fractured, deep and private parts of themselves, and to know their value.

I have the power to change the trajectory of a person's life. We all have that power; to be kind, to have compassion for others and essentially, to be a blanket in someone's snowstorm.

Amy Hall

Amy Hall is a proud mother to two beautiful autistic children, wife to an incredible partner and a successful, passionate business owner in regional New South Wales, Australia.

Amy is a teacher, youth mental health advocate and child and adolescent behaviour support practitioner. She has earned multiple university degrees in education, leadership, youth work and mental health advocacy, and is currently working on her second master's degree in disability policy and leadership. With a career spanning over twenty years, Amy has established herself as a trusted advocate and leader in supporting vulnerable populations and promoting social inclusion.

Amy is the founder of Banksia Support Services which was inspired after Amy delivered a beautiful baby girl at twenty-six weeks gestation in the middle of the pandemic. The experience of 107 days in hospital watching her daughter fight to survive taught Amy about resilience and inspired her to follow her passion and be the captain of her own ship.

Since the business' opening in May 2021, Amy has supported over three hundred families across Australia which involved supporting children who live with complex disabilities who demonstrate unsafe behaviours because they are unable to communicate their wants and needs in ways that others can easily understand. While business was never her life's mission, she has excelled and won multiple awards being recognised as both a business and disability leader in her community.

Amy's work includes supporting parents and key people in the child's life to understand how to promote quality of life and safe behaviour, while empowering the child to develop their own unique identity and communication preference. Amy's mission is to promote understanding about her clients, who they are, why they behave in different ways, and how their community can maximise their quality of life through skill building and proactive supports and reduce the need to restrict or restrain them (in Australia this is known as a reportable restrictive practice).

Amy also consults with multiple government organisations across Australia in best practice approaches to support children with disabilities when they come to hospitals, attend school communities and when they are transitioning to work. Amy is passionate about sector capacity building. She is the clinical supervisor to forty-five behaviour practitioners nationally. Most recently Amy has developed and implemented a national training program for behaviour practitioners which is aligned to the Australian National Disability Insurance Scheme (NDIS). This is one of the first of its kind in Australia to date.

Amy believes in the two degrees. That her work can shift a trajectory of a person's life just enough that if she succeeds, she can positively influence their future long after they exit her service.

Amy lives with disability and has always needed to work hard to retain information and has learned to navigate significant barriers with numbers and reading, but this effort has been the bridge to overcoming great adversity and modelling for others how disability does not have to be a barrier to success, achievement or being a leader.

PURPOSE & PASSION

Facebook: facebook.com/banksiasupport
LinkedIn: linkedin.com/in/amy-hall-banksia
Website: banksiasupport.com.au
amyhall.com.au

Life is a Journey

Embrace the Experience

Arusha Pather

DEDICATION

To my parents: Thank you for having the courage to leave your families to find your purpose and follow your passion.

To my kids: Thank you for being mine. I love you to the moon and back, and back again.

To my husband: Valleys and mountains are much more interesting than smooth lakes. Thank you for travelling with me on this journey.

To my 'Girls and Boys': Dreams and hard work go hand in hand. Dream big, you can do anything you put your minds to.

To all those who have influenced and guided me on this path, I am thankful for our interactions and life experiences we have shared.

'In the end, we only regret the chances we didn't take.'
– Lewis Carroll

PURPOSE AND PASSION

If I were asked about my purpose in life or my passion during my teenage years, I would have been at a loss for an answer. At the time, I lacked the life experience needed to determine the direction I wanted to take, or the significant accomplishments I hoped to achieve. The one thing I was certain of was my desire to assist and support others. This is still a life principle I strive to uphold. The prospect of a dynamic work environment with direct interaction with people appealed to me more than a sedentary office position and led me into the health care sector.

My career pathway became clear to me during the second year of studying for a bachelor's degree in radiography. As student radiographers, we were tasked with learning about diagnostic medical imaging techniques such as X-rays, CT scans, MRI, nuclear medicine and ultrasound procedures. One particular moment stood out to me. While observing an ultrasound examination in a dimly lit room, I watched in awe as the sonographer guided the probe over a patient's stomach, revealing a detailed image of a baby on the monitor. Witnessing the movement of the baby and hearing its heartbeat left me fascinated. The sonographer was experienced, and her passion for her job was truly inspiring to me. I was amazed at the precision and wealth of information she gathered about both the mother and unborn child in such a brief time frame. During the following weeks of this placement, I experienced both the joys and sorrows associated with obstetric scanning. The more I learned and the more hands-on experience I gained, the more determined I became to pursue a postgraduate diploma and specialise in ultrasonography.

Despite encountering a few obstacles and deviations along the way to becoming an accredited medical sonographer in Australia, my focus in obstetric sonography led me to attain a master's degree in medical ultrasound. My enthusiasm for this field was further encouraged when I was granted the chance to establish my own 3D/4D ultrasound studio and radiology clinic. Witnessing the delight on the faces of new patients as they catch a glimpse of their baby for the first time brings me immense joy. I see it as an honour to be part of one of the most precious moments in their lives and I am dedicated to ensuring this experience is as magical as possible.

LIFE IS A BOOK

My parents belong to a generation where life was tough, both geographically and culturally, to pursue their dreams in their home countries. They had the courage and determination to leave their families and friends, venturing overseas to seek opportunities and careers that were not readily available to them back home. They crossed paths in the UK in the 1970s, my mother had moved from Mauritius to study nursing, while my South African-Indian father was studying optometry.

Growing up, my brothers and I spent our childhood in South Africa and our early adulthood in the UK. From a young age, our parents instilled into us a deep appreciation for academia, influenced by their own experiences and cultural norms. It was always expected we would complete our education and pursue university degrees. My mother's words still ring true for me today: *Knowledge is a valuable asset that no-one can take away from you. Use it to be self-reliant and shape your life on your own terms.*

This can be applied to any academic level, as, in my opinion, the most valuable knowledge we acquire stems from interactions with others who have shared similar experiences, rather than solely from books or formal programs. I have always advised new students to fully embrace their training period. The undergraduate program should be a time for exploration, where asking silly questions and making mistakes are all part of the learning process. It can be as enjoyable as you make it, as you and your cohort are likely to cross paths in your professional careers later, particularly in a niche field like sonography. Building a positive network, with peers who understand your professional journey, is beneficial. I feel that postgraduate or advance studies serve the purpose of refining and honing your skills. They enable you to cultivate and amplify your inherent abilities, preparing you to deliver the highest level of service in your field.

My academic journey to my current position has been a convoluted one, taking me through various challenges and experiences. Upon completion of my radiography studies in the UK, I made a significant life change by moving to Perth, Australia. The degree I had just completed allowed to me gain employment within two weeks of my arrival. However, finding a training position for sonography proved difficult, as new graduates were encouraged to gain at least two years of clinical experience before pursuing postgraduate studies.

Undeterred, I returned to the UK to pursue my postgraduate studies. Upon my return to Australia, I faced difficulties in converting my qualifications to Australian standards as, at that time, most international radiography degrees were recognised but postgraduate sonography diplomas were not. I eventually re-enrolled in an Australian program to retake my practical exams. It was particularly difficult securing a training placement due to the somewhat exclusive nature of the sonography profession.

Training positions were typically offered to existing staff members, leading to long wait-lists and limited opportunities for externally trained candidates like me. After briefly returning to radiography and contemplating abandoning sonography entirely, I found myself at a low point. I was deeply disheartened and frustrated by the scarcity of opportunities and lack of assistance in my field. However, my fortune changed when I landed a job at an independent radiological clinic run by a radiographer who had the vision and strength to open his own clinic, at a time when, historically, radiology clinics and departments were run by doctors. The professional support I received there was a lifeline during a time when I was feeling both professionally and emotionally depleted, and I will always be thankful and grateful for the opportunity.

LIFE IS A CHALLENGE

My transition from a clinical worker to a business owner evolved naturally when the chance arose to establish my own 3D ultrasound studio, which later expanded to offer X-rays and diagnostic ultrasound examinations. After nearly two decades of experience in radiography and sonography across hospital departments and private clinics, in both urban and rural areas, I had a wealth of experience and knowledge to draw from.

The decision to establish my own practice was not straightforward. With three young children in primary school and a background focused on clinical skills rather than business and management, I had to reflect deeply on my decision and consider how it would impact my young family. However, I couldn't ignore the promising opportunity and hope to inspire and motivate my children through my choice, just as my parents had done years ago when they left their hometowns in search of career opportunities.

As I worked through the necessary legalities, registrations and accreditations needed for setting up a medical practice, it became evident that few sonographers have taken this path. The majority of departments and clinics were overseen by radiologists (medical doctors) or health care business corporations, most of which were not forthcoming with advice or guidance.

I confronted this challenge by ensuring I was equipped with the necessary knowledge. I researched and reached out to networking contacts and professionals in the field for advice and guidance, gradually obtaining all the required accreditations and authorisations. Determined persistence is essential when venturing beyond conventional practices as, along the way, obstacles and diversions are inevitable, and how you handle them shapes your advancement. You must forge ahead independently to drive progress, and at times it is necessary to pause, reassess and regroup.

My biggest challenge, by far, was changing my mindset from a clinician to a clinician/business owner and to promote the advancement of the business. Building up a reputation for high-quality diagnostic scans and patient care was essential and central to gaining the trust of the referring clinicians, thus, promoting referrals into the practice.

LIFE IS SORROW

An aspect of obstetric sonography frequently underestimated is the reality of infertility and pregnancy loss. Experiencing infertility or the profound loss of pregnancy is an indescribably painful and isolating experience. Feelings of inadequacy and guilt can be overwhelming in the harsh reality of unfulfilled dreams and shattered expectations. In these moments of sorrow, it is challenging to see a way forward or find solace. The pain of infertility or pregnancy loss cuts so deep that it can shape your perspective on life and motherhood.

As a woman who faced infertility, underwent IVF treatments and encountered pregnancy loss, I have been tested to the brink of my emotional strength in this realm. I have experienced a spectrum of emotions – from sadness, unfairness and anger, to relief, joy and happiness.

By embracing meditation and reiki healing practices, I immersed myself into, and acknowledged, each sentiment I felt. In this way, I was able to overcome feelings of grief and sadness and journey on towards healing and hope.

Recognising the emotional toil these experiences can have on women is crucial in creating a safe and understanding space where they feel heard, validated and supported. Offering a listening ear and comforting touch, without judgement, can make a world of difference in helping women cope with the uncertainty and emotional turmoil that can accompany infertility and pregnancy loss.

I have come to understand that each woman is embarking on her unique pregnancy path, and as a health provider, my role is to walk alongside her, offering support and guidance as she intuitively connects with her pregnancy experience.

The most rewarding moment of my day is when I have the privilege of reassuring a mother that her baby has a heartbeat. In that moment, the joy and relief washing over her face is a reminder of the incredible power of life and the beauty of motherhood. Witnessing the emotions of hope and excitement at the sound of that tiny heartbeat is a truly heartwarming experience which never fails to move me.

LIFE IS LOVE

I have been truly blessed to have a supportive family and friends in my life. My husband's support during the most sorrowful and challenging times of our lives has been invaluable and essential in bolstering my path towards healing. My family's unwavering love and encouragement have also been a source of strength and comfort for me during these times. Their presence in my life is a constant reminder of the importance of surrounding oneself with positive and uplifting people.

My pregnancy journeys have given me three beautiful children and a wealth of experience. I have gained more strength and resilience watching and supporting my children grow up. They constantly inspire me to do better and remind me of the importance of striving for excellence in all aspects of life. During my toughest and most exhausting moments, they uplift and support me with the same words of encouragement I impart to them. This motivates me to push myself beyond my limits and set a positive example for them.

LIFE IS ADVENTURE

Life is a grand adventure that must be embraced to discover our true purpose. If I had succumbed to the initial obstacles of establishing my own business, I would have missed out on the sheer delight of sharing precious moments with parents and their unborn children. Reaching the stage where you can fulfil your work purpose while indulging your passion turns past setbacks and let-downs into mere memories.

The real challenge lies in advancing the business while remaining faithful to your vision and principles. Both you and your business must evolve continuously to adapt to new innovations and concepts. There is immense joy and excitement in experimenting with a novel technique or product and witnessing their success unfold. Ensuring you remain up-to-date with evolving technologies and protocols is also crucial for both professional and personal growth. Knowledge is still your most valuable asset.

The best advice I can offer to a young person is to discover a purpose or career pathway that promotes a feeling of responsibility, fulfilment and satisfaction from a job completed well. Begin by creating a list of preferences for your dream job such as: indoor or outdoor work settings, travel and career advancement opportunities, sedentary office position or energetic work atmosphere, internationally recognised qualifications, specialisation in a particular field and remuneration considerations. This will assist you in refining the possibilities and professional pathways open to you.

The drive to reach new heights will naturally emerge when the time is right. As your purpose and passion align, your life's journey becomes significantly more gratifying and can pave the way for a richer existence, both personally and professionally.

LIVE YOUR LIFE
Life is a book – study it.
Life is beauty – worship it.
Life is a challenge – meet it.

ARUSHA PATHER

Life is a dream – realise it.
Life is a tragedy – face it.
Life is a song – sing it.
Life is love – enjoy it.
Life is a game – play it.
Life is adventure – dare it.
Life is a promise – fulfil it.
Life is sorrow – overcome it.
Life is bliss – test it.
Life is a duty – perform it.
Life is a journey – end it.

Arusha Pather

A rusha Pather is a highly skilled medical sonographer with over twenty years of experience in radiography and ultrasonography. She is the founder and director of Roselea Imaging services and The Baby Scene 3D Ultrasound Studio. Arusha is deeply dedicated to the field of sonography, delivering exceptional patient care and top-notch service.

Arusha, the second of three siblings, was born in the UK to a South African-Indian father and a Mauritian-Indian mother. At the age of three months, her family relocated to South Africa where she spent her informative years immersed in the diverse cultural landscape of KwaZulu Natal. In the early 1990s, the family moved back to the UK to pursue work and education opportunities, transitioning to a nuclear family structure. Balancing an eastern cultural upbringing with a western social environment, Arusha navigated her teenage years in the UK, attending Esher College in Surrey before pursuing a BSc (Hons) degree at South Bank University. After completing her degree in radiography, she made a life-altering decision to move to Perth, Australia.

Arusha obtained the challenging diploma of medical ultrasound

(DMU) from the Australasian Society of Ultrasound in Medicine (ASUM) in 2008. Throughout her career as a radiographer/sonographer in urban and rural settings, both in private clinics and hospitals, Arusha continued her educational journey, culminating in the completion of her master's in medical ultrasound from Charles Sturt University in 2013.

In her personal journey and development, Arusha is grateful to be the mother of three wonderful children. She found solace in meditation and reiki healing during the most challenging times of her life. This experience inspired her to complete Reiki I and II of the Usui Shiki Ryoho Reiki practice, becoming a practitioner of this healing art since 2016.

Currently, Arusha also holds a sessional academic position at Edith Cowan University in Perth, where she shares her expertise with future ultrasound trainees and conducts professional development courses. Her commitment to educating and mentoring new graduates is evident in her work as she strives to inspire and empower the next generation of health care professionals.

My Ancestor's Spirit Within Me

Bernice Hookey

'When you do things from your soul, you feel a river moving in you, a joy.'
– Rumi

T his is my story ... Leaning in, I close my eyes, listening deeply to the stories of my ancestor's survival. Sitting around a campfire, under a gum tree by the river, or at the table with a cup of tea and biccies, I remember listening to Mum speak about the strong matriarchal women, and the strength of the men, in our family lineage. This is what gives me the fire in my spirit, stoked bright, to keep from entering the dark where I once drifted away and got lost.

The story told is so powerful in its truth-telling. For it is those stories about my Old People, the grandfathers and grandmothers, which give us a deep sense that being grounded in their roots and connection provided for their commitment to self-awareness, and my reflection for care and connection, in such a profound way. That reflective learning meets the needs of exploration and context to relationships, adopting the dismissed opportunities to feeling joy and healing, in place of trauma, that generational trauma has disempowered growth for happiness and a happier future.

I find it important to listen deeply to their stories and the many stories of Elders today, for they are part of our future and our children's future, the history of the lands we are connected to, the footprints we leave behind and the people we meet.

It wasn't easy when I first put pen to paper to write down in my journal how I was feeling, having experienced the deep cut of words that felt stuck to me like a stain, or entered my soul like a poison to disempower me or dismiss self-love. Having the words flow out onto the page felt surprisingly good, as it's not always easy to express and share feelings, even on paper in a journal. Back in my Old People days, they expressed themselves through storytelling, without knowing that reflecting on their time, when sitting around a campfire or having bottomless cups of tea, for that is what they did, is a form of self-care and self-love. My story of purpose connects through the millions of tears I cried and the circles I have sat in, as I know my soul is healing, and the ripple effect to impact change is on the horizon.

There were times when I questioned my worthiness, my ability to stand up for myself, waiting for permission to do so. I've since learned that I unintentionally abused my own self-confidence and self-control, denying myself self-love or the ability to build up confidence and self-esteem. Why do we do that to ourselves? It was not, by any means, the fault of my Old People, it was the way of life; not knowing that to take care of myself first was a selfless act. To teach is to learn and to learn is to teach. There was not always that opportunity; there was only ever survival. I may not know all the answers, but what I do know is the answers I projected to tell myself were that I do not need permission to just survive and to speak up for myself. When I am being brave and courageous, even through tears that fall or emotions stuttering my voice, I shed light on learning from experience. Indeed, the experience took me back to times when my Old People had no choice, whereas today, the choices we make can bring back joy and healing to the soul.

So, to you, the reader, be open to taking carriage of being uncomfortable and take a moment to sit and listen, deeply listen, to the Old People's (in your family or elderly strangers) stories, for their stories are what gives them a little more time here to share and takes them back to their youth. Though, for me, those stories take me into the future, to not just survive, but to thrive. For if we do not make the time to show up for them, how can we stand up, speak up and own it, to honour our own voice; to echo loud and proud, that their voice is now our voice. Remember, you are a voice for the many who are still finding their way; finding their voice in amongst the dusty roads, the muddy waters or the overgrown bushes and the crap that seems to either feel like it's too much to navigate through, or the crossroads you will come across in your way. Know this; the dust eventually settles and the mud does dry up. When you use the right tools to clear the bushes and use the cow manure for fertiliser to sow the seeds, this is the start of new beginnings. But don't go backwards or turn around at the crossroads, always take a left or right to keep moving forward. New beginnings don't have to start when the new year rolls around either. They can start at any time you are ready to create something new, closing chapters that no longer have a purpose for you.

I created my own way when I came across obstacles.

I used the cow manure that had piled up (metaphorically speaking) and took a shovel and spread it, so I could make use of it and 'grow through what I go through'. I took on the learnings of the stories from my Old People and went on the path of accepting that the only person who can help me – is me. That is, to focus on myself first and to love myself, so I can prepare myself physically, mentally, emotionally and spiritually, so I am ready for this new beginning and new chapter on my journey. Every day is preparation day, not just for when I participate in or complete a course to do better, but an everyday practice of self-care. It is not just smelling the roses for the smell to overpower the crap in my life, it's what has been that gives me the hope and passion to drive change. The cow manure smell will go away because I can take control of what I am going to do with it. I will use it to grow the roses! Don't underestimate the power of what cow manure can do to turn a brown patch into greenery. Hence, take that crap and spread it like fertiliser!

The words of international motivational speaker, Lisa Nichols, resonated with me … 'No-one else is my rescue; I AM MY RESCUE.' There are days when I do feel alone, and there are days when that feeling of loneliness can invite in unwanted stresses. But I have been able to handle them by reminding myself that it is a moment, and that loneliness is a mirage, not an image that is seen. Fear is another unwanted stressor. Being afraid can lead to numbness and isolation. When I have been absent from myself, my soul has no joy, no happy hormones, so no love to nourish it. Noting that, I surround myself with many circles. These can range from circles of influence to circles of connection, to people to simply connect with, for when we find the right 'circle of people', we begin to glow like glow sticks!

When I can step into my story and share it out loud, it truly does feel less of a load. When it is not shared or spoken about, I know it can weigh you down. I found my way, through the storytelling of my mum sharing about the Old People, and the power in being fearless can unpack masked pain and open a clear path, paving the way to breathe in fresh air, not the toxins that can either slow or deteriorate my motivation, or my mind, to move forward. To cleanse the soul is to honour the tears and let them fall freely.

It is so refreshing when I allow the tears to flow out of my eyes freely, without feelings of judgement or shame, especially when I am sharing with an audience. I entered the year 2024 with one word on my mind: *abundance*. For no matter what obstacle I faced, I made a choice to choose a meaningful purposeful word, that if I embrace with a passionate heart, I am allowing the soul to transform the river of blood through my veins to be enriched with the love and care my physical, mental, emotional and spiritual presence so deserves. What is in my control is how I can fuel the passionate light of living and live it with empathetic actions and a grateful heart, to nourish the mind with beauty within, so that love is abundantly idolised in a way that only you know the feeling. You know the path to creating the beautiful bed of your favourite roses, or flowers, to flourish and grow abundantly from the fertiliser you used, to give life to the soul.

I cannot express enough how life lessons and learnings of deep listening can enrich the mind; the deep listening to the stories of my Old People has restored connection for my body, physically, mentally, spiritually and emotionally, and gives hope to the spiritual essence for the energy to always recharge. Knowing my surroundings and knowing my very reason for sitting around a campfire, taking in the smell of the smoke and reflecting how smoking the body over is a sacredness towards caring for self and caring for the betterment of each other.

Place your hand over your heart and close your eyes, gently letting the sun kiss your face. Breathe in and breathe out three times. Do this to awaken the senses, and don't forget to drink water and welcome the new day. It is a new day because every day is a new opportunity to start afresh. Take small steps, even if it is one day at time, for this has been my way of making an impact, to improve my love for myself, to give love and show up, leaving a ripple effect of inspiration and healing power to release, recharge and restore the energy, to fill up our cup and top up love in my heart, soul and mind. When I look into the mirror, I talk to my reflection to tell her three things to start the day. I say powerful words to remind myself I exist. I remember to say it with love and conviction to feel the thrill and adrenaline rush within me, to feel the shift in the strength in my words, and the feeling of the strong woman I know I am. I start my day with saying hello to that beautiful woman I am looking at in the mirror. But remember, don't think about what you want to say, just let it flow! What I choose is thoughts that work for me:

1. I AM Bernice Hookey (Say your name). 2. I AM proud of YOU (smile and point at the mirror – see your reflection for your eyes to light up). 3. I AM love. You can choose what you like; these are examples of how I start my day for the woman I am looking at in the mirror. Words she deserves to hear.

A favourite song by pop singer Michael Jackson is 'Man in the Mirror'. The lyrics are powerful, suggesting that change starts with us. I can confidently look at that woman in the mirror knowing that her healing has been an everyday journey, and she is making a change.

This small start to the day, or any time of the day, has helped me with adopting the practice as part of my self-care, so that the stories I continue to share around the campfire, the table (at home or work), under the gum tree by the river or with my circle of people, is my abundance.

'The abundance of the universe is available to everyone.' When I opened myself to the potential of receiving the flow of abundance, it touched something deep inside my soul; the river, the joy.

In all my travels, the journey always led me back to trust the process; trust in the Ancestors' spirit energy, that bleeds out what is no longer accepting. Acknowledging and deeply listening to the stories told and hearing the once-silent voices now echoed through the channels of the riverways and the wind whistling. Feel the breeze cool you, the rain wet you and take note of Mother Earth speaking up, that when the story I share gives a sense of belonging to self, the flow of healing is trusting the power within me, guided by storytelling and stoking the fire within me, to keep burning the flames to light the way.

My courage isn't the absence of fear, it's the decision to act despite it. And if my voice echoes in the wind through the rustling of the trees, you can deeply listen to the message and together we can know we are seen. When I know I contribute to the story, the healing will be the change needed for a thriving future for all, for my future, my children, their children and my Ancestors' and Old People's stories.

Reflection is a journey, and one I know. If I compared myself to where another is going, I learned to not lose focus on the *totality of possibilities,* and that you can start at any time in life. Another affirmation I stand by, '*comparison is the thief of joy*', from Theodore Roosevelt – that is my purpose and my passion is always to love on myself, to give back love.

Oprah Winfrey is an incredibly inspiring woman for many people around the world, and it is these words she shared that compliment my journey and the spiritual connection to my Old People and storytelling: 'If you're willing to listen, guided by that still, small voice that is the GPS within yourself, that makes you come alive, you will be more than okay. You will be happy; you will be successful, you will make a difference in the world.'

With love,
Bernice XO

Bernice Hookey

Bernice, a proud descendent of the Waanyi People in the Lower Gulf of Carpentaria, Queensland, and on her maternal grandmother's side Murrawarri People in northern NSW, is on a mission to add value and increase people's culture to transform inclusive representation and visibility in presence and voice for Indigenous People, in the construction and mining industry, organisations, government (local, state and federal), private sector and foreseeable future globally.

Bernice is mum to her children and two fur pets, an accomplished speaker, author, mentor and leader. She has held roles in senior management directly reporting to general managers, CEOs and successful family business operations, five- to six-figure budget projects and founded several businesses. Bernice is an advisor with a board responsible to contribute towards consumer health, a forum on issues of strategic significance in the provision of quality health care to Aboriginal and Torres Strait Islander consumers and provide advice to organisational decision-makers. Bernice sits on advisory boards for James Cook University JCU College of Business Law & Governance (CBLG) and Townsville University

Hospital.

Bernice provides a unique, culturally safe environment, accountability, tailored design and the mentorship you envision to achieve change and transform into the cross-cultural exchange as at the same time respectful boundaries. She's like the transformation scout challenging community innovation.

Bernice is a survivor of disempowerment, feelings of unworthiness, wellbeing depreciation and has overcome little or limited opportunity in any prevention into the culture of the right to speak up. Bernice has lived it and experienced it, and has gained skills in experiential learnings – that's where her learnings and experience come in.

An alumna of Murra Indigenous Business Masterclass Program, Melbourne Business School, a former student of Tranby, a Fellow of the Australian Rural Leadership Foundation flagship program and recognised inspirational and influential leader for North Queensland, Bernice learned new business skills and enhanced her confidence as a leader by learning alongside other Aboriginal students and highly regarded leaders from around the country. A past member of the Communication Reference Team (CRT) of the National Rural Women's Coalition NRWC.

After completing her studies, she embarked on a journey of leadership and founded MZB Empowerment to improve the quality of life for Mob. She is a voice for the voiceless. She is also the principal consultant of Bernice Hookey Consulting. BH Consulting is a niche professional service established as the next step to generational equity. It is a regenerative development initiative formed on the basis that Sovereignty of Australia was not ever ceded, it is a function to work with Aboriginal and Torres Strait Islander communities to create First Nations Community Land Trusts (CLT).

The flagship 'Modern Matriarchal Care' serves as a unified voice, First Nations CLTs are structured with Indigenous design and development education for their community.

Bernice seeks to strengthen the empowerment of individuals through unique program delivery in a culturally safe environment. Bernice is committed to walking in solidarity with Mob and allies along their leadership journeys and supporting them to thrive.

mzbempowerment.com.au
bernicehookeyconsulting.com.au

THE MAGIC OF MINDSET IN ENTREPRENEURSHIP

Candice Wilson

From the day I entered this world, I've always had a natural passion and love for animals. As a child, you would see me with our dogs, cats or mice, dressing them up and pushing them around in prams. I'm fortunate to live my life with purpose each day, and in this chapter, I'll take you on my journey of the power of positivity and the magic of mindset in life, business and being a mum.

I have the ability to shift and stay in a positive mindset – 98% of the time. I am grateful I was given a strong desire to lead and have the drive to stay focused and achieve my goals.

It hasn't always been this way though. I must admit, I've had my struggles and hurdles during my youth and early twenties after my parents separated. I finished high school in year ten and went to boarding school in Armidale – it wasn't for me. When I reflect on my life, I always knew I wanted to work with animals and be a veterinary nurse. With my love for animals and an amazing work ethic, I started my career in the pet industry at the age of fourteen, surrounded by purposely driven veterinarians and nurses. It is such a positive and inspiring industry.

I always spoke of one day having my own doggy day care, an ethical pet care business serving hot lunches to dogs, which back then, was not a thing. This brought so much joy and direction to my life but when I was away from work, I struggled to shift my mindset and focus on my identity and the path I knew was best. I had my share of partying and working in night clubs as a second job to support myself. I moved out of home at eighteen, moving in with my brother, before venturing into my own flat above the chemist at Drummoyne, the following year, with my two domestic short-haired rescue cats, Kyah and Teetree, as well as my tropical fish. I've always had animals wherever I lived.

I come from a family of entrepreneurs, two older siblings and high-achieving parents; my dad with a love and passion for electronics and the security industry running their own business called Altronics in western Sydney. We were raised in the control room of a leadership environment, as well as observing their drive and commitment to their passions. This contributed to my work ethic and I'm forever grateful this has provided me the natural ability to take on leadership and management roles. My grandad owned and led multiple boating and pool companies; Osprey motors, Champion pools and Mariner Outboards, to name a few. I also have an uncle who has established, led and listed multiple mining companies on the stock exchange. So genetically, both sides of my family are strong-minded, focused and gifted entrepreneurs.

My mum always encouraged us to *be us* and supported us to achieve our highest potential, guiding us to our purpose. I'll never forget the day I'd worked a long shift at a bar the evening before, sleeping through my alarms I needed to get to the city in time to enroll myself at TAFE for veterinary nursing. My mum went all the way into the city on a rainy day, walking through puddles, to ensure my enrolment was submitted on time. She knew working with animals was when I was at my happiest, and she guided me through the tricky teen years.

I try to see the best in everything. I want to see people smile and live their best lives. Having such passion, purpose and positivity has now brought me to leading a team of thirty people and running a successful pet care business.

We are all human and can all have off days; can you relate when you're having one of *those mornings,* when you spill the milk, kick your toe on the door jamb or lose your keys? You start to think ... *Why me? Poor me. This always happens to me!*

But when you have a magic mindset, you can shift, laugh it off and correct those feelings and thoughts, knowing this happens to every single person once, twice, a hundred times or more, in their lifetime.

What makes the moment magic is the ability to shift from missing to magic – and guys, this is one of the biggest powers any of us can take into each and every moment. I can think of so many times in the nine years of business where I've had those moments, and they could have been life-changing. Those moments could have had the ability to put a stop to achieving my goals, but the magic of mindset changed everything.

You can shine by creating your circle of like-minded individuals and leading a life that practices gratefulness, journalling your daily wins and acknowledging the lows but always pushing through the tough times. If I can share and inspire you with my greatest wins, it would be accepting the noise and those negative thoughts; be proud of *YOU,* love *YOU.* Acknowledge you and you have one amazing life, and we are all put on this Earth for a purpose.

'Find your why, your purpose with positivity and together we can all make magic.' – Candice Wilson

In January 2012, I met my now-husband, Andrew. I was working night shifts as an emergency and critical care vet nurse, still working within the vet industry. I knew I needed to do something else with my big dreams, goals and the desire to one day have my own business. With my entrepreneurial spirit, stemming from my upbringing and my high-achieving parents, I was still searching for my WHY, even though I was working with my passion and purpose. Lost and still searching for my complete identity, I had decided to do a bachelor of nursing. I was in my final year of an accelerated course doing pracs, when I found out I was pregnant. To our surprise, our beautiful son entered the world. Moving in together with no savings, getting to know each other after only dating for four months, our beautiful little Wilson family journey began. My identity became clearer and my WHY was being a mum as life started to flow outside of work. Waking up each day, knowing my identity was fulfilled and my WHY was complete, I had found the missing piece to my puzzle after all those years. My beautiful children and family ignite my drive and push me to be the best version of myself.

Do you wake up each day and promise yourself you will be the best version of you?

Do you only want to speak positively about life, manifest your dreams and nurture everyone around you?

If you don't, that's okay, but try doing this as a daily practice and see what feelings this brings to your life, your business and family. For me, I know it makes me strive to be the best version of myself and have a magic mindset, which helps in every aspect of my life.

Starting Bloomingtails on 19 November 2015, I remember people commenting, 'You're going from an emergency and critical vet nurse to a dog groomer?' Lots of negative talk and comments. Belief and bravery came a long way. I'm sure many of you reading this now have experienced this one way or another.

I started my business at the rear of the vet hospital at Riverview, establishing my clientele through letterbox drops and pushing brand awareness to the locals. No uniforms and documenting appointments, and data was on manual system cards and a diary. Every day I had focus and a strong desire to provide the highest standard of ethical care to all the dogs and their owners. Courageous and connected to my business are some attributes I am proud I take into every day. Waking up to my WHY drives me high.

Starting the business while being a mum, I had even more purpose. My identity was now complete, and I was happy. It doesn't matter what we do, if we develop a product, provide a service or ecommerce business, it's the passion, purpose and finding your WHY that will motivate you to strive and shine. Another magical milestone: Andrew and I welcomed our beautiful daughter in 2020.

'Purpose directs passion and passion ignites purpose.'
– Rhonda Britten

I believe each and every one of us were put on Earth to make a difference, to make an impact, and I hope my chapter ignites and inspires you to manifest and continue to aim for your dreams with a positive mindset. I am very grateful I've had this opportunity to share my biggest belief in leading a business and life and achieving one's goals that we can all do. I am an *all-or-nothing* sort of person in everything I do, which can sometimes be sacrificing, but I always circle back to gratefulness which then aligns me to make a difference.

I believe what you speak is what comes to you and what you manifest also flowers. Goal-setting and journalling gives me direction. I always listen and am extremely intuitive to signs in my life. I kept having the same name come into my life and I analyse things like this as *nothing is a coincidence.* By being intuitive and connected spiritually to oneself this has now opened a massive new chapter in my life and I am forever grateful for this gift. Be intuitive, be connected and conscious to the things around you and follow your intuition and light will guide you.

'Have courage and be kind.' – Cinderella

I have learnt over the years how important it is to nourish my body. Eating well and exercising daily is a huge part of my ability to stay focused on my mindset. Like anything, it is a practice, and routine is key. I run 5-10km most days, but there are some days I don't feel up to it. There are days I get to 3km and want to give up, but I never do. I push through the thoughts and always say I CAN, I WILL, I'LL CONQUER and feel amazing at the end.

'Nothing is impossible; the word itself says I'm possible.'
– Audrey Hepburn

I will leave you with a daily practice that keeps me aligned and makes me love, appreciate and experience a day of gratitude and happiness.

Morning gratefulness practice:

I am grateful for my family … I am grateful for my friendships/ partner/husband … Because … I am grateful for who I am because … Something I am grateful for today is …

Something funny I am grateful for is …

Something else I am grateful for is …

I also like to take this practice to our dinner table in the evenings for the whole family to share one thing they are grateful for that day. It's such a special practice and keeps so much joy within our little family.

How would you feel if you did this practice every day?

PURPOSE & PASSION

'There's a spark in you, you've just gotta ignite the light and let it shine.' – Katy Perry

With love and inspiration. Keep shining, everyone. Candice xx

Candice Wilson

This chapter is dedicated to my beautiful mum Trudi Aitkens
Thank you, Mum, for giving me life and always being such a positive
light and energy and answering my fifty calls per day and believing
in me. I love you.
To my two beautiful children, Jett and Ayla, thank you for giving me
so much purpose in my life.

Candice Wilson is an award-winning entrepreneur and mother of two. The founder and CEO of Bloomingtails 2015, a leading pet care business that was built with passion and purpose, with two locations, offering seven amazing services. Candice loves nothing more than empowering ambitious individuals entering the pet care industry and mentoring them with over twenty years in the industry and a strong commitment to animal welfare and ethics.

As a certified emergency and critical care veterinary nurse and certified dog groomer she brings a wealth of knowledge within her industry. Nothing brings her more joy than seeing dogs live their best happiest lives, their owners smiling and leading a team of like-minded dog enthusiasts. She opened her doors to provide the highest level of ethical care and commitment to each and every pet and their owner and is proud to say they achieve this every day.

Having experienced a life of purpose and passion with animals from a very young age, Candice shares her journey in life, business and being a mum. The magic of mindset to achieve goals including some of her daily practices to living a joyous life.

If you're reading this book you're most likely an entrepreneur with big dreams and Candice hopes this chapter ignites and inspires your journey with entrepreneurship.

'My creativity in this chapter is here to ignite and inspire you.'
– Candice Wilson

Website: bloomingtails.com.au
Email: candice@bloomingtails.com.au
Instagram: @bloomingtails_dog_grooming @bloomingtails_farmstays

Affirm Your Potential

Dr Marie Anderson

'Purpose is the reason you journey. Passion is the fire that lights the way.'
– Author Unknown

I was about twenty-seven years old when I first asked myself: *Who am I?* I thought I knew.

I had just been promoted to personnel manager at the head office of a large, well-known corporate company, a role I'd been working towards since my early twenties. When I arrived at my new office that first morning, I felt so happy. I went about making the office my own; a few books here, a couple of garden-picked flowers there and placing my stationery exactly where I wanted. I stood, initially admiring my newly acquired workspace. But then something came over me – a sense of emptiness. As I stood there, staring blankly at the wall, I felt nothing, nowt, zilch, nada. In that moment, my purpose for my job felt passionless.

Research[1,2,3] shows that if we have a sense of purpose, we may have a healthier, happier and more fulfilling life. We may be less stressed, less anxious and less depressed. In addition, if our life feels purposeful and has meaning, we may feel more passionate about the things we do. How cool is that!

However, life doesn't always occur that way automatically. Although our sense of self, purpose and meaning develop over time, our early life experiences shape our reality and how we feel about our lives. We are influenced by our observations, what people think and expect of us, how others reward or discipline us, how we compare ourselves with others, and what we hear people say about us. These experiences provide the reasons which give our lives purpose and meaning, whether they are real, imagined, positive or negative.

Through sharing my personal story in this chapter, my aim is to inspire what might be possible beyond our circumstances, hopefully to a future marked by vigour and intention. That's not to say that anyone's circumstances *need changing*. Or that people are unhappy or passionless with their lives now. No, not at all. Our lives can be full even in the most challenging situations and conditions.

I hope to offer some insights about finding purpose and passion, even a little, in areas of life that feel stagnant and stuck. We will explore ideas that generally hold us back and those that propel us forward. I will also provide some reflections at the end to ponder the main points of the chapter. Hopefully, the ideas discussed here will inspire some to begin or continue along a purposeful and passionate journey.

SUPPORT: Should anyone read something here that raises difficult memories or emotions, I encourage and professionally recommend seeking support from a friend, a family member or a professional health practitioner. Although it may seem we are alone in our struggles, I hope my story provides a sense of courage to source strength and comfort in those who can reassure us.

EXPECTATIONS OF SELF

'What you think, you become.' – Buddha

When I had those thoughts in my office, all those years ago, I didn't understand what the feelings meant. They confused me. Here I was, having been offered the role I'd worked so hard for, and all I felt was a void. Curiously, my mind asked me, *Is this it? Is this who I am?* I recall thinking, *What the hell! Where are those thoughts coming from?* At the time, I ignored them. I simply got on with the job. That's what you did. You get on with what's expected.

I was raised in a strict Italian Roman Catholic family. The expectations were clear; you study hard, you work even harder and you make something of yourself. Don't get me wrong, there was lots of love, laughter and, of course, celebrations with food aplenty – haha. But duty, contribution, hard work and gaining approval from others was what it was all about.

What I know now is that who I was becoming was a conglomeration of my cultural, religious and societal expectations. That wasn't so bad. The values I was raised with have set me up for a productive life – respect for others, strong work ethic, family first, punctuality and so forth. But I knew from a young age that, somewhere inside, there was more to who I was than the expectations imposed upon me.

Expectations are the *musts*, the *have-tos*, and the *shoulds* in our life. They are the rules by which we learn how to behave in our community, workplace, family and the world in general. These beliefs guide and direct us to ensure we make it to where we are going. As useful as expectations are, they can often keep us trapped in limiting dialogue about our sense of self, keeping us ambushed in a passionless and purposeless life journey.

The expectations of self I have learnt over the years helped me explore my potential in the corporate workforce and the community I was raised in. These expectations steered me forward in predictable, unsurprising, knowable ways. As long as I worked hard, did what I knew pleased others and stayed steadfast, I would be applauded and, inevitably, validated. I was becoming who I thought I wanted to be, only to realise that who I was becoming was a superficial, ideological self.

DECISIONS VERSUS CHOICES

'It is our choices ... that show what we truly are ...' – J K Rowling

Don't get me wrong, I loved my corporate life – right up until I didn't. I had chosen my destiny in human resources. I had chosen to study management. I had chosen to be where I was going with my life and career. But had I really chosen?

As I became more unhappy and dejected with myself, I started questioning my choices and decisions. As if dissociated, I became aware of saying *yes* to things when I actually meant *no*. I became aware of undertaking activities that were manoeuvring me towards a future that didn't feel intuitively *me*. I saw that my decisions were not choices. My choices were actually decisions.

Generally, I think we take for granted that decisions and choices are the same. And from a certain point of view, they are. But I would argue that they differ.

My trusty old Oxford Dictionary[4] defines a decision as a 'conclusion, formal judgement; making up one's mind'. It defines choice as 'of picked quality, exquisite; carefully chosen, appropriate'. My take on the Oxford definitions is that decisions are about coming to a resolution and choices are selectively perceptive.

My aim here is to draw attention to the differing distinctions. I believe a decision is a process of weighing up pros and cons that can be based on entrenched expectations.

Whereas a choice is more likely based on some intrinsic awareness, insight or knowing that the preferred option is the undeniable action or solution forward. I'm not saying choices are better than decisions. Absolutely not. I'm simply drawing a distinction that might help release us from limiting assumptions.

All my life I was making decisions. Unconsciously analysing the good and the bad, the right and the wrong of every move I made. But the decisions were based on pleasing others, looking good, not making mistakes, avoiding conflict, dodging judgements and seeking reassurance that I was perfect. Sound familiar?

Whereas, when I started making conscious choices, my potential, of who I felt at ease with becoming, flourished. Initially, I struggled between the decisions and the choices. My automatic need to process and analyse was too forceful, even too enticing. The fear of doing something wrong or insulting others through my actions was overwhelming.

However, slowly and surely, by navigating the choices that intrinsically made sense to me, I began to design a life that felt more real than what came before.

MEANING OF SELF

'I wonder what's possible if I think: I am enough!' – Marie Anderson

Fast-forward beyond that purposeless moment in my corporate office, I came to learn that my defined sense of self, which gave my life meaning, was based on who I thought I was supposed to be, rather than who I truly can be. This insight occurred to me after embarking on my own developmental journey. With time, education and awareness, I came to see that creating a meaningful, passionate and purposeful life required stepping outside of my comfort zone.

At the point when I distinguished this insight, I faced some very scary options. I was proposing to myself that I quit my secure, comfy, very well-paid corporate job to go and do what I had been procrastinating doing all through my twenties. That is, study psychology.

However, at the time, it felt out of my reach. I believed I wasn't smart enough to sustain the years of study. I had always been good at academia, until year twelve when I didn't get the usual high marks. I thought I'd finally proved what a flake I really was. In reality, my mother had been unwell during that time in my young life, and it distracted my commitment. But I was eighteen – what else would I think? The meaning I applied to my year twelve experience hindered my self-belief.

Years later, when I became aware of the self-defeating belief that I was not good enough to pursue my chosen career, everything in that moment made sense. Everything about who I thought I was became clear. I was impelled forward in my life by a definition of myself that subdued my full potential to go to university, be a psychologist and have a private practice. So, I focused on what I believed I was good enough for in life. I was oblivious to these limiting beliefs that contributed to my self-doubt. I was inadvertently keeping myself small to keep myself safe from being imperfect.

Through my developmental journey, I came to define myself by my strengths and values rather than my deficiencies and inadequacies. I reconstructed my meaning of self. The meaning we apply to who we are will inevitably show itself in our beliefs and behaviours; meaning influences the perception of self. Change the meaning, change the outcome of self.

THE UNKNOWN SELF

'One is never afraid of the unknown, one is afraid of the known coming to an end.' – Jidda Krishnamurti

In reconstructing my belief of self, by my early thirties I was faced with excruciating fear. The idea that I could quit my expected life to design one that was unfamiliar with an unknown outcome scared me intensely. Despite the fear, I was pregnant, with a three-year-old and a husband, who was also venturing into new horizons. *Holy moley! What would people think? How would we survive financially? What if I failed!? Bla, bla, bla, bla …* you get the picture.

The unknown is a very scary place. As humans, despite the fact we may seek out the adventure of the unknown, we essentially live within the known because it predicts survival. If we consider moving into the unknown, then our stress response may be activated. That is, our fight or flight mechanism. The brain may say something like, *Hey, what are you doing? Where are you going? There's danger out there in the unknown.*

You might get killed, or ostracised by your tribe, or maimed, or fail along the way. Stay on the known path. Don't veer from what's recognisable. Stick with what you know.

That fearful voice in our head is a very strong, very powerful, very unrelenting mouthpiece. And rightly so because it is trying to keep us safe. The stress response is an important part of our survival, so we want it to be automatic. However, we want to begin harnessing our rational mind to choose what is and is not technically dangerous. Yes, we might make mistakes. Yes, we might be judged. Yes, we might even fail. But for the most part, these experiences teach us lessons and move us closer to affirming our potential.

The truth is, people did think I was nuts. We were financially strapped, living on credit for many years. But we did survive. I'm not going to paint a rosy picture; those study years were gruelling. I studied full-time, while financially I had to work casually, and shared the child-rearing with my husband (thanks, Peter). Making the unknown a known experience was taxing. We were fortunate to have support from my parents who, to their credit, despite wanting to have me psychologically evaluated in those early years into the unknown, were there for us. I also must mention my bestest and dearest friend (hi, Margaret) whose support I could not have done without.

THE AFFIRMED SELF

'If all difficulties were known at the outset of a long journey, most of us would never start out at all.' – Dan Rather

If I'd known what I was going to be up against to get to where I was going, I might have never started down the path in the first place. There were twists and turns, there were tears and rants, and there were moments I very nearly gave up, if not for the commitment and passion that drove me to realise my purpose and potential. Oh yes, there was another best friend who spurred me on at the eleventh hour when things seemed relentless (thanks, Natasha).

In any event, the unknown eventually became the new known. I came to see that that is how it works. One day you know yourself as the expected self, and then another day your purpose becomes affirmed. During the arduous journey of growing into myself, I learnt to appreciate, admire and accept who I was becoming; warts and all. It gave me a sense of optimism and ease. I saw myself transform from an irrational self-defeating being to a rational self-affirming one. My self-worth was thriving.

I truly believe that because I was following who I was intrinsically becoming, the road felt familiar, despite the obscurity. It's as if I was being pulled and propelled forward to a calling that felt reassuring.

I had uncovered my purpose. That is, to inspire others to grow their potential to live a balanced and meaningful life. In my role as a psychologist, I found meaning by contributing through my therapeutic work. Interestingly, I had always been enthusiastic about sharing wellbeing knowledge and supporting people to change. So, in some way, I feel that our purpose is within us; experience and awareness may guide us towards its emergence.

FINDING PURPOSE AND PASSION

So, where to start? There are many ways forward. My experience and what there is to learn here is one way. It is not the best way or the only way. It is *a way*. I have always encouraged people to read widely, seek trusty support openly and immerse themselves in healing therapies and developmental workshops.

I've come to learn that purpose and passion may grow incrementally through the accumulated effect of life experiences. For some, this might be a vocation, for others a hobby, family, a new idea, travel, parenthood, volunteering, a quiet life, achieving daily objectives, lifestyle change, supporting a cause and so forth. Purpose can appear in many guises.

I end with a reflective summary of the ideas raised throughout the chapter. My experience suggests that the journey to fulfilment is rarely easy or straightforward. But, by taking small steps, we move closer to realising our goals and intentions.

Explore the expected self, be conscious of decisions versus choices, identify the meaning of self and ride the wave of the unknown self so it becomes known again. The evolution of who we are becoming allows our purpose and passion to unfold and be affirmed.

REFLECTIONS: INTRODUCTION

- We might be happy and yet still feel empty.
- We might achieve our goals and still feel unfulfilled.

- We might be exactly where we think we want to be in life and still lack purpose and meaning.
- Purpose provides the reasons that may ignite passion, which propels us forward.

REFLECTIONS: EXPECTATIONS OF SELF

- Confusion and curiosity might be a precursor for insights and change.
- Our expectations of self may be influenced by our life experiences.
- These expectations serve us well to grow and follow through with our community standards.
- Expectations might contribute but also may impede our sense of purpose.

REFLECTIONS: DECISIONS VERSUS CHOICES

- Decisions provide a helpful analysis of pros and cons, dos and don'ts, rights and wrongs. They are judgements often driven by expectations.
- Choices provide solutions often based on inherent values and intrinsic beliefs.
- Both decisions and choices are valuable approaches to creating forward movement.
- Purpose and passion may be inspired by integral actions of our potential.

REFLECTIONS: MEANING OF SELF

- Our meaning of self is influenced by who we think we are, the good and the bad.

- Education and awareness may reshape our meaning of self.
- Fear and self-defeating beliefs can be powerful killjoys.
- Our strengths and values define us more potently than our deficiencies and inadequacies.
- Finding purpose and passion might be possible if we challenge our comfort zone.

REFLECTIONS: THE UNKNOWN SELF

- Failure can be a gift to learning and change.
- The unknown provides an opportunity to grow.
- Stress may play a part in our adventure to fulfilment; harness it constructively.
- The lessons we learn along the journey may inspire our potential.
- A trusty support network is imperative to sailing through a purposeful and passionate life.

REFLECTIONS: THE AFFIRMED SELF

- Focus on the solutions for now, not the difficulties to come.
- The unknown might be scary but in time it becomes the known.
- Appreciate, admire and accept who we are becoming.
- Acknowledge the thriving self-affirming transformation.
- The purpose and passion inside of us may emerge with awareness and action.
- Purpose may inspire passion, which can propel our potential.

REFERENCE LIST

1. Boreham, I.D., & Schutte, N.S. (2023). The relationship between purpose in life and depression and anxiety: A meta-analysis. *Journal of Clinical Psychology, 79*(12), 2736-2767. doi.org/10.1002/jclp.23576
2. Schaefer, S.M., Boylan, J.M., van Reekum, C.M., Lapate, R.C., Norris, C.J., Ruff, C.D., & Davidson, R.J. (2013). Purpose in life predicts better emotional recovery from negative stimuli. *PLoS One, 8*(11): e80329. doi:10.1371/journal.pone.0080329
3. Sutin, A.R., Luchetti, M., Stephan, Y., Sesker, A., & Terracciano, A. (2023). Purpose in life and stress: An individual-participant meta-analysis of 16 samples. *Journal of Affective Disorders, 345*, 378-385. doi.org/10.1016/j.jad.2023.10.149
4. The Concise Oxford Dictionary of Current English (5th ed.). (1964). London: Oxford University Press.

Dr Marie Anderson

Dr Marie Anderson is a clinical and health psychologist. She has an interest in the natural therapies and takes a holistic view of emotional wellbeing. She has a degree in the behavioural sciences (psychology) with honours, is a fellow member of the Australian Psychological Society's Clinical and Health Colleges, and is a registered psychologist with APHPRA.

All through her twenties, Dr Marie aspired to study psychology. However, her self-defeating beliefs held her back. By her early thirties, she had embarked on her study journey, registering as a psychologist in 2004 and then graduating as a doctor of health psychology in 2012 at La Trobe University, Australia. As a therapist, she is passionate about supporting people to grow their potential so that they learn to live a meaningful and balanced life.

She has a long history in human resources, training, occupational rehabilitation and health psychology at a leading general hospital. Her doctoral thesis explored the use of motivational strategies to support effective health behaviour change. Dr Marie also completed additional training through Deakin University to provide clinical psychology services.

Dr Marie has an established health clinic in Melbourne, Australia, that offers a number of supportive modalities. As a holistic therapist, she believes that the mind and the body need nurturing for optimal wellbeing. She offers in-clinic and online therapeutic support, and her aim is to evolve her practice to offer online programs. She also has a newsletter that offers helpful health hints.

Dr Marie says that her top accomplishments are completing her doctorate, contributing to the emotional development of her clients and, most importantly with her husband, raising two adaptable, amazing men.

After feeling unfulfilled with corporate, Dr Marie commenced private practice in 2004. She knew that she wanted to make a difference to people's lives by supporting their emotional growth. Because of her own journey, she feels particularly inspired to help her clients deconstruct well-meaning limiting dialogue that keeps them feeling stuck, empty and unfulfilled.

Using evidence-based techniques, she supports her clients to grow their potential by helping them identify what's possible, as opposed to living a life from who they think they are, based on life expectations. She provides education and strategies to help them cultivate affirming beliefs, nurture their strengths and live by their principal values so that they can perceive a stronger sense of meaning, purpose and passion in their lives.

The work Dr Marie does with clients is integrated, eclectic and strategic inside of the therapeutic model. Despite the fact that many people seek out support because they are unhappy, she often says to clients that if happiness is our goal in life, then we will find ourselves forever chasing moments upon moments of *happy*. This searching can be draining and dejecting because life can be full of *down in the dumps* experiences.

So, her aim with clients is to encourage them to be adaptable and resilient so that they can traverse life's ups and downs constructively. In doing so, she believes they move in the direction of fulfilment given that realising one's potential is often an exploratory journey to who we are becoming.

Website: balancedwellbeingcentre.com.au
drmarieanderson.com.au
facebook.com/drmarieanderson
instagram.com/drmarieanderson

Forget Toxic Productivity

Three Tools For Thriving From Burnout

Dr Olivia Ong

There are many reasons why you might be reading my book chapter right now. Although each person's reasons are unique, they often fall into one of three categories, driven by some core frustrations you may be experiencing.

The first frustration may be that you are feeling overwhelmed and exhausted from juggling it all. Pressure from work and home, managing expectations and everyone else's needs, the kind of exhaustion from carrying the mental load that leaves you emotionally spent, finding it hard to laugh or find joy.

The second frustration might be that you're tired of overthinking things and want to powerfully address that thought-feeling loop. You long for greater emotional mastery and the skills to shift your emotional state anytime, anywhere.

The third reason you might be here is because you struggle with knowing what you really want, you lack self-trust and are indecisive, or repeatedly give your power away to others.

With our always-on, always-available, fake-it-'til-you-make-it hustle culture, there's glory in being the workaholic, the go-getter, the workhorse.

We've normalised hustle culture and made it that if you're not always busy and stressed, you're not trying hard enough.

Answer an email late in the evening. Sure! Put in extra hours on the weekend? No worries – you didn't have plans anyway.

Being stressed and overworked is a toxic mindset that keeps you pushing harder and harder, until you end up in burnout. But once you recognise it, you can prioritise self-love and break the toxic productivity cycle.

WHAT IS TOXIC PRODUCTIVITY?

In recent years, our culture has been about the hustle and the grind. The *first-in, last-out* type is the one who gets the promotion.

The shift to hybrid and remote work only worsened this mindset. The boundaries between our work and our personal lives blurred more and more. Our phones and laptops are always on, we're always available – and *expected* to be.

It's difficult to turn the notifications off, especially with no physical separation between work and home. Our home office, couch, recliner or even our beds may have become the new workspace, so *of course* we can't just turn our work-minds off.

With no rest, no downtime and no boundaries, we can't enjoy our free time or focus on self-care and self-reflection. We may prioritise a project over date night, our child's sports game or recital or even sleep.

Productivity is important, but it can be detrimental if it consumes our lives. If we think work is more important than anything else, to the point where we can't relax and enjoy our families, hobbies or time spent on our own, that's when productivity builds to burnout.

Balance, rest and self-love are vital to true productivity. If you're running on fumes, are you truly productive? Is the work you're doing the best quality it can be?

Probably not.

MY STRUGGLE WITH TOXIC PRODUCTIVITY

'Love what you do, and you'll never work a day in your life.' We've all heard some variation of this quote, implying that if you're passionate about what you do, it will never *feel* like work. You can't get overworked, stressed or burned-out doing what you love, right? *Wrong!*

I was nearly claimed by my own toxic productivity. I worked all the time. Sadly, I was addicted to being productive – it was my badge of honour.

Then COVID-19 hit. The lockdowns, stillness and claustrophobia of the pandemic made me feel I had to move faster, produce twice as much and push toward my ultimate goal.

I was buried in toxic productivity without realising it – only to be buried by the bad-news avalanche. In fact, I was burned-out.

Burnout is essentially what happens when we try to avoid being human for too long.

I've spent a lot of time working with people, including medical professionals, to tackle burnout. During that time, I discovered there are three core problems of burnout:

1. Exhaustion.
2. Depersonalisation.
3. Lack of self-efficacy.

People often talk about 'beating' burnout, 'stopping' it before it starts, 'curing' it and even just 'surviving' it.

But as individuals, we can't stop, beat or cure burnout. It isn't a personal failing, something we can switch on or off based on our personal choices alone. It's a result of broad systemic issues way beyond our control.

In fact, a 2023 Women's Agenda Australia study showed that major factors leading to burnout in the workplace include discrimination (13%), challenges with management (34%) and pay disparity (26%).

My background is in the medical field, where at any given moment, over 70% of practitioners are experiencing burnout – and more than half of those burned-out doctors, nurses and staff are women.

But it's not just the medical industry. People, especially women, are suffering from burnout in everything from hospitality to legal practice.

We can't eradicate burnout, but what we can do is slow it down.

WHAT IS THE ORIGIN OF BURNOUT?

Burnout isn't new. Back in the 1970s, researcher Christina Maslach constructed a twenty-two-question survey that became known as the Maslach Burnout Inventory, or MBI. The MBI identifies three symptoms of burnout:

1. Exhaustion: You're extremely tired and unable to recover. Things are either chronically miserable or on a downward trajectory.
2. Depersonalisation: This is an unfeeling or impersonal attitude towards the people you are meant to serve. In short, you just. don't. care. Your ability to empathise nosedives.
3. Lack of self-efficacy: This manifests when you begin to doubt the purpose of the work you do and stop believing in yourself.

HOW TO THRIVE FROM BURNOUT?

Let's think about burnout in terms of three core energy accounts, like a bank account for your brain and body. These 'accounts' correspond to each of those three symptoms we just looked at.

PURPOSE & PASSION

1. Exhaustion and your physical energy account.

We all have a physical body, and we must take care of it. When we don't sleep and eat poorly, or work too many hours – especially if we're sitting at our desk the whole time – our physical energy account gets overdrawn, and we experience the first symptom, physical exhaustion.

2. Depersonalisation and your emotional energy account.

The next symptom is depersonalisation, when you just stop caring. When your emotional energy account has a low balance, likely because your own emotional needs aren't being met, you just can't be emotionally present for others.

You can fill this energy account by finding time for the important relationships in your life. Are you spending enough time with the people you love? For most high-achieving professionals, there is a huge imbalance between the time you spend working and the time you would like to spend with your children, friends, significant other and family.

3. Lack of self-efficacy and your spiritual energy account.

When you lack self-efficacy – when you stop believing in yourself, your work and your purpose – you need a big deposit to your spiritual energy account.

When I talk about spirituality, I'm not just talking about any type of religious practice. If you have a religious practice that comforts you, please keep it up. But when I use the word 'spirituality', I'm talking about your week-to-week connection with a sense of purpose and meaning in your work and your life. You make a deposit into your spiritual energy account whenever you experience a connection between what you're doing and your purpose. These experiences could be coaching your children's soccer team, volunteering to teach kids to read, overseas medical missions or anything else that feeds your spirit. You can structure your life to increase the frequency of these experiences too.

MY EXPERIENCE WITH BURNOUT

Like most people, my burnout happened gradually. From my childhood as an academic overachiever, to striving to walk again after a devastating spinal cord injury, to pushing hard throughout my medical career, my whole life was constant strain.

And in 2019, I fell flat on my face. This time it wasn't because of my legs – I was in throes of severe burnout. I was exhausted, I had insomnia, and my usual bubbly and optimistic attitude had diminished into cynicism and sarcasm. All of my three core energetic bank accounts were overdrawn.

At the time, I was working full-time as a pain specialist. I'd just finished three gruelling years of studying for my pain fellowship exams – what in the US they call board certifications – and I was juggling being a mother to a three-year-old boy while navigating my physical disability. People would say, *Wow, you must be superwoman,* or, *I just don't know how you manage it all.* The truth is, I didn't know how I did it either.

My energy and wellbeing reached dangerously low levels. The combination of all these demands had exhausted me. That was an overdraft notice from my physical energy account.

I started withdrawing and disconnecting from the people around me. I was cynical and sarcastic towards people – a message from my emotional energy account.

I wondered how much longer I could go on like this, barely holding it together at a job I no longer felt passionate about. I felt disconnected from my purpose as a doctor – a warning message from my spiritual energy account.

All three of Maslach's symptoms showed up for me. All three of my energy accounts were in the negative.

I had visions of the physician and the mother I wanted to be. I wanted to work the hours I desired in my clinical practice and spend quality time with my son, Joe. I knew there had to be a way where I could build my career – and feel good about it – while growing my family. Surely, there had to be a way for me to become the leader and mother I envisioned, without the physical, emotional and spiritual exhaustion of burnout.

My story of recovery from burnout started from a place of basic human needs: to learn how to care for myself, then to care for my family and provide for them. If I wasn't okay, we weren't okay.

From that point of falling 'face flat' from burnout the only possible way was up. I had to recover from burnout and figure out how to make burnout work *for* me in the future.

Burnout working for you instead of against you. What?

See, we're getting closer to the *joy* of burnout.

I realised three things:

1. I needed to be 100% responsible for myself. There were lots of things I couldn't control – big, institutional, systemic issues. But I could control my own choices.
2. It was time for me to up the ante on self-compassion.
3. To gain wisdom and learnings from my burnout experience, I would have to *appreciate* the burnout. Ugh, I know, right? But it's true.

These three personal development power tools, which can be described as self-empowerment, self-compassion and self-appreciation, taught me how to thrive at home and in my medical practice.

HOW TO OVERCOME TOXIC PRODUCTIVITY WITH THE THREE PERSONAL DEVELOPMENT POWER TOOLS

The most important tool for overcoming toxic productivity is knowing how to recognise it.

- Are you always focused on work? Always checking email on nights and weekends, even during time with your family or friends?
- Are you measuring your self-worth through your work? Is excelling at your job or career the most important thing to you?
- Are you missing out on quality time with your family, friends, pets or hobbies in order to work?
- Are you using work to escape difficult life situations, such as a significant death or conflict with your partner?

If you answered 'yes' to any of these, you may be struggling with toxic productivity.

Fortunately, you can break the cycle of overworking.

You can use the three personal development power tools of self-empowerment, self-compassion and self-appreciation to reconnect and recharge, focusing a little on yourself. It is time for a reset, my friend.

SELF-COMPASSION: TAKE AN EXTENDED RECESS FROM WORK RESPONSIBILITIES

If you've been going and going, it's time to be compassionate towards yourself and take a break. Spend time recharging and reconnecting. Feed your soul, reflect and reset. Rediscover a lost hobby or take up a new one.

Go for a walk or a drive with no destination in mind. Lie in the grass and watch the clouds. Do the least productive things you can think of to give your mind and body a rest.

However you choose to spend your time, it's important it's about what *you* want, not the professional *you*, but the personal *you* – the multifaceted *you*.

Over time, you'll get used to unplugging and enjoy some much-needed time for yourself.

SELF-EMPOWERMENT: PRIORITISE WORK-LIFE BALANCE

Even if you work from home, you need to empower yourself to create clear boundaries between work time and private time. You can set a work schedule for yourself, much like office hours, or designate time slots when you can be productive, working around your family's schedule.

Whichever you choose, it's important to stick to your schedule. Adjust as needed but be disciplined in your work time *and* your personal time.

During your personal time, do the things you enjoy. Practice your hobby, spend time with family, cook yourself a meal, watch your favourite television show, meditate – whatever makes you happy. When you return to work, you'll be refreshed and ready to go.

SELF-APPRECIATION: CREATE A SELF-LOVE TOOLBOX

We all need reminders to develop healthy habits and appreciate the things we love about ourselves; and the self-love toolbox is just that. Having a self-love toolbox on hand can reinforce the message and give you tools to prioritise yourself.

Drawing from my experience as a wellbeing and thought leadership business coach, I put together a self-love toolbox that has all the tools and resources you need to love yourself greater! I'm always telling clients to create flashcards for their positive affirmations, and now I've taken that idea ten steps further to build the ultimate toolkit so you can end your toxic productivity.

END THE TOXIC CYCLE WITH SELF-LOVE

Toxic productivity can sneak up on you, but when you know what to look for, you can promote better work-life balance and unplug to unleash your true productivity. When you can overcome the three symptoms of burnout by making deposits to your three energy accounts, you can slow down burnout, keeping you healthy longer, developing more time, freedom, better work-life balance and becoming significantly more connected to your life's true purpose.

If you enjoyed my book chapter and you would like to know more about the topic of burnout, you can sign up for my newsletter on my website: drolivialeeong.com

Dr Olivia Ong

Dr Olivia Ong is an esteemed pain and rehabilitation physician, and an expert in burnout and resilience. She is also an international award-winning bestselling author, TEDx speaker, global keynote speaker, award-winning physician entrepreneur and health care thought leader.

In 2008, after a life-altering accident, Olivia was told she would never walk or practice medicine again. After years of recovery in hospitals and rehab facilities in Australia and the US, she won the battle to walk again and even resumed her medical career. Today, she shares her journey to motivate and inspire others.

Driven by her experience, Olivia now works as a coach and mentor for doctors dealing with burnout. She has also authored a number of books, including the international bestseller *The Heart-Centred Doctor*. With her son, Joseph Lee, she published an enchanting children's book, *Jo-Jo the Kind Sloth*, which encourages children to cultivate resilience and see the world around them through new eyes.

With her unwavering determination, profound insights and

compassionate spirit, Olivia is sharing her secrets to unlocking the power of self-compassion and overcoming adversity.

Birthing Business

Lessons from Motherhood

Emily Mitchell

It was 9pm, the night before my son's first birthday. I was swearing and on the verge of tears as I was making his cake. The icing wasn't cooperating, and the picture in my head compared to what I had in front of me couldn't be more different. Motherhood, anyone? I had put so much pressure on myself for the cake to be homemade and perfect, which represented how I wanted to be portrayed as a mother. What I didn't know then was that I was chasing an impossible standard.

At the party the next day, as everyone was celebrating my son and we cut the cake, I just thought, *What about me?* I'm the one who grew, birthed, fed and nurtured him. I'm the one who kept him alive and thriving for a year and my prize? A barrage of stress from the birthday, where my effort and sacrifice over the past year wasn't even acknowledged. It was my birth-day too after all. I began to wonder if this was how all mums felt and decided we deserved to be reminded that we matter too.

I was motivated to make sure mothers felt celebrated and validated. That we were thanked and recognised for the crucial work we do every day. I committed myself to bettering women's motherhood journeys and, as a new mum, birthed my business to gain some control and make it happen. While there isn't a lot of control in motherhood, I soon found many similarities between birthing and nurturing a baby versus launching and running a business.

IN THE PRE-CONCEPTION PHASE, WE PREPARE

It's in this phase that ideas and intentions are born. It's often from pain, wants or needs. Any good business solves a problem, otherwise there's no demand for it. There are practical problems to fix, like creating shoes to protect feet, but there are also emotional or psychological problems to fix, like supporting mothers to feel seen and valued. Consider what problem your business idea fixes and how it can make people feel. That's your selling point. Test it with family, friends and anyone else in your network to see if there's a demand.

Hand in hand with this is your WHY. Your WHY is the reason behind your business. It's important to have a strong WHY behind what you do. It gives you purpose, passion, direction and motivation during the good and the bad days. It's easy to find your WHY when what you want is a future baby. You're already wired to give them the best possible life, and that starts before they are even an embryo. In business, it can be a bit harder to find and maintain that strong WHY. To find your WHY, ask yourself – *What do I want this business to achieve and why is that important?* And keep asking. Dig deeper, until it makes you emotional.

Use your story to fuel your WHY. My story started on my very first day of maternity leave at thirty-seven weeks and three days. I stood up from the couch to put a plate in the sink after dinner and felt a gush. Initially, I thought it was my waters breaking, but when I went to investigate all I saw was bright red blood. Flooding out. I rang the hospital and told them I was coming in. The midwife on the phone sounded indifferent, which foreshadowed how I would be treated within the health system. I had had a partial placental abruption, which led to an emergency C-section and a postpartum haemorrhage. While I was on the table in theatre, I felt like an afterthought. No-one acknowledged the incredible transition from maiden to mother that had unfolded. It felt like I was only there so they could pluck my baby out. Then, I was discarded. My experience was not seen as important, and this thought bled into a depleted postpartum period where I was taught the only thing that mattered was my baby. But I decided mothers matter too and chose to educate and empower women and their families, so they didn't have the same experience. Why? Because mothers are as vulnerable as their babies and they deserve to be held just as tight.

In motherhood, our WHY is rarely us, but I urge you to include YOU in your business WHY. My business was born from my own lacklustre introduction to motherhood. I believe I deserved a better experience, that **all mums deserve a better experience,** and I don't want any other mum feeling unappreciated, alone or overwhelmed. So I did something – for them – but also for me.

What's your story and your WHY?

IN THE PREGNANCY PHASE, WE GROW

Ourselves, mainly – but our business too. In this phase, the seed is planted and it's our opportunity to develop it. This is where we expand our idea and get clearer on what our business looks like and how it will operate. It's like writing a birth plan, but as well as including what you want to happen, and how you will get there, you can also include how you want to feel throughout the process and ways to make that happen. Personal development is key. Expand what you think is possible by immersing yourself in worlds that support your dreams.

It's important to understand what success feels like to you and make plans towards that. Put your blinkers on and don't be sidelined by society's expectations of what success looks like – the corner office or the white picket fence might not be your cup of tea. Authenticity is key here because even if you achieve things other people deem successful, if it doesn't mean anything to you, it will eventually feel empty to be validated by others but not yourself. Check in with yourself often to see what is motivating your decisions and adjust accordingly.

This phase is an opportunity to do the work to understand yourself – what lights you up? What drains you? Be open to opportunities that align with that. There might be hiccups and discomfort that you weren't expecting, but accept that growth comes from being uncomfortable. New awareness is where we learn to trust ourselves. Understand as much as you can about yourself and the business world, so you know your options and where to turn for help, because we all need support sometimes.

IN THE BIRTHING PHASE, WE COMMIT

It's go time! In this phase you might be going live, launching websites and opening for orders. It's exciting and nerve wracking. You might feel relief or trepidation or excitement. You know that (birth) plan you wrote? Expect complications. There's always something that pops up to scare you or unravel your best made plans. That's okay – this is where we learn. Welcome it. Life would be boring without growth, and mostly everything is manageable.

Birth is usually the focus of motherhood and launching is the focus of business. While it's so important to be informed and know how you want it to look and feel, including who is around and the outcome you want, the birth/launch is just one important step in the journey. As much focus on the birth/launch needs to go into everything else afterwards as well.

When a baby is born, so too is a mother, so when a business is born, so too a businesswoman. Who we are evolves. I've found the focus is not so much about retrieving who you were before, but on who you are becoming. The things you discover about yourself and the world, and the parts you choose to keep and nurture or reject and release, become you. When you are committed to becoming and connecting with yourself, you can't help but grow – and so too does your impact. Hold and honour yourself throughout this journey just as much as you hold and honour your children.

Ask yourself – *If I take away motherhood or business ownership – who am I? What do I value? What makes me feel alive? What answers does my body have?* This is your true north, and you deserve to be spending your time on it. Try and incorporate a little bit of it into every day and prioritise your joy. How you feel matters. Your experience matters.

Take time to pause at this milestone and acknowledge your progress. We often steamroll on to the next thing but it's so important to stop and celebrate your achievements; all the blood, sweat and tears. You birthed a business, you put yourself out there and now the journey really begins.

IN THE POSTPARTUM PHASE, WE NURTURE

This is where we are at our most vulnerable. We have shared our creation with the world and the ball is in their court. Orders and enquiries might fly in, or they might not. In this phase, we nurture our creation, learn and try new things. We fall, we get back up, we recover. We learn the value of patience and perseverance, while we try and regain balance in our lives.

I'm sure you've heard that it takes a village to raise a baby, though often that village is non-existent in modern society. The good news is we can build a village, in motherhood and in business. Collect people who support you, guide you, people who have walked the path before you and can provide advice so you can bypass lessons learnt. You might be tempted to do everything yourself in the beginning to save money, and I get that, because I thought the same. I did it all – tried to build my own website, tried to cold call potential stockists, tried to manage all my social media, tried to write all my own newsletters, do my own branding and graphic design, tried to learn SEO, tried to manage marketing – all of it while being a mum to a toddler and working part-time in a corporate job.

All aboard the burnout train. I quickly found that some parts of business just don't light me up, and if engaging people who love those parts is an option for you, it might lift some weight from your shoulders and free you up to enjoy the experience. I have made some incredible connections with people who have supported my business and allowed me to focus on relationship building and income producing activity that lit me up. When your energy is high, you'll attract more of that positivity and opportunity into your life. While it's in this phase we realise we need a village, try to build your support early in the growth stage.

In motherhood, there are no awards and little, if any, recognition of a job well done. But in business, there are plenty of awards to enter to gain that feeling of satisfaction. Going through an award application process is such a valuable experience, and not just for your ego, but for your confidence. Taking time to reflect on your business journey, all the connections and progress you have made validates your growth and achievements. Research the awards available in your industry and throw your hat in the ring. It gives you credibility and content for your website and socials. You may also meet incredible people with opportunities for collaborations and general hype-girl support. You will never regret an award you enter.

Don't be afraid of failure in this time. Give yourself permission to fail. Release the fear and accept it as part of the process. Release the need for perfection and it will give you freedom to try things you might not normally. If something isn't working, pivot. Take what you have learnt, try something else and grow your confidence. You'll soon become the person you need to be to realise your vision of success.

We all know it's easier to stay in our comfort zone. I feel resistance every day to progressing my business because my prehistoric brain thinks, *Woah we haven't done that before! What if you get rejected? You could die!* We're not living in the same world we were back then though. Our brain thinks sending an email poses the same threat as a tiger chase. We must acknowledge these fears, thank our brains for keeping us safe, the best way it knows how, and then choose another way through another thought and action.

The journey of birthing and nurturing anything is ever evolving and individualised. That's the beauty of it. How it looks for me and you could be completely opposite and that's perfectly okay. Do not compare. Trust in where you are going and why you are going there. Celebrate yourself and your growth often. Focus on how far you have come instead of how far is left to go.

Remember, the world is designed for men on their twenty-four-hour clocks, but we women have a twenty-eight-(ish)-day clock; we are made to operate differently. We are cyclical beings, and our intuition is incredibly powerful. It's hard to decondition the way we've been raised to exist, but this is your journey, on your time line, in your way. Only you can deliver and nurture your baby or business in the way it needs to be. Trust yourself.

When I started my business, I thought I needed control, but instead, I found purpose. I uncovered, and continue to discover, who I am and just how worthy I am of the same love and attention that I, and everyone else, freely gives to their children. That's my hope for you. That your business or baby elevates you into a more aligned and evolved version of yourself, where your worth isn't questioned.

What started as a meltdown over a birthday cake, turned into an opportunity to highlight injustice and get people thinking differently about motherhood. Maybe you can have your cake and eat it too. Just make it is store bought to save your sanity.

KEY CHAPTER POINTS:

- Similarities exist between birthing and nurturing a baby and a business. Don't buy into society's unrealistic expectations of enjoying every minute of motherhood or business – some parts are hard and unenjoyable, but there's always a way to figure it out, even if you can't see it straight away.
- Prepare – Test your business idea and figure out why it's important to you and others.
- Grow – Develop your idea and yourself. Understand where you are going and how you are going to get there. Build your village.
- Commit – From womb to world, we birth our idea. This is only the beginning and time will bring clarity. Be easy with yourself while you navigate a new identity and reality.
- Nurture – This is where the real work begins as you grow alongside your creation. Vulnerability, fear and failure will be a part of your journey – embrace them.
- A healthy baby/business, a healthy mother/businesswoman and a healthy experience are all important. You are unique, as is your worth and impact. Honour your own individual journey.

Emily Mitchell

Emily Mitchell is here to disrupt the motherhood narrative. She believes mothers deserve a better experience and is committed to helping others help mothers by having open conversations about parts of motherhood usually hidden. Emily believes that every mother's story is unique and the more we share our realities the less alone others feel, the more we learn and the more we normalise the wide range of experiences in motherhood.

Founder of Motherhood Milestones, Emily creates heartfelt cards for real-life mums that promote education and empowerment. She has created a mainstream way to facilitate conversations and change the way people think about motherhood. Every Motherhood Milestones card has a magnet on the back so they can live on the fridge and an affirmation on the front that she hopes reminds mums, every time they go to the fridge, just how important they are.

Emily is a keen advocate for mothers and has partnered with government to improve their experience. She is the co-chair of the Maternity and Neonatal Consumer Reference Group with the Agency of Clinical

Innovation (ACI) and member of the ACI Maternity & Neonatal Network Executive Committee, working to improve families' experience in the NSW Health System and beyond.

Alumni of the inaugural 2023 Kindlab initiative run by the NSW Ministry of Health, Emily pitched the Honouring the Fourth Trimester Program idea because she doesn't want any other mother having an unsupported and overwhelming postpartum experience like she did. The program was selected, has funding allocated and will be further developed and implemented over the coming years.

Winner of the 2023 Women with Altitude On My Way Award, Emily is committed to growing herself and her business and continuing passionately on her journey to remind mothers that they matter just as much, if not more, than their children. Emily believes that while a healthy mum and healthy baby are important, so is a healthy birth and postpartum experience.

After feeling like a burden at her own birth as a mother and wanting no other mother to feel the same way, Emily is passionate about reducing the isolation mothers feel. Rejecting society's unrealistic expectations of motherhood, Emily freely shares her experience to normalise the real motherhood and help mothers feel less alone.

Mother to her son Lincoln, Emily is grateful for motherhood as it continues to teach her so much about herself and the world – often bringing up thoughts and feelings that would not have been worked through otherwise.

Emily has worked in local and state government, the not-for-profit sector and private industry. Now an entrepreneur, Emily enjoys leaning into what lights her up and making an impactful difference to women's motherhood journeys.

Emily is a lifelong learner and has a Bachelor of Communication, Master of Arts in Journalism and a Graduate Diploma in Ethics and

Legal Study. She has also been initiated into the Usui System of Natural Healing (reiki).

Website: motherhoodmilestones.com
Instagram and Facebook: @motherhoodmilestones

From Baby Loss to Business Growth

Navigating Grief and Resilience in Entrepreneurship

Georgina Windebank

NAVIGATING GRIEF AND LOSS IN THE FACE OF DAILY TRIGGERS

The irony of losing three pregnancies and then working with pregnant women is not lost on me. A cruel blow enforced by the universe without understanding why. A slap in the face, way too often for it to be forgotten and for me to be 'over it' as society and so-called friends have said I should be. Slashing at my heart each time with their insensitive words and assumptions of the time frame in which these agonising losses should be *no longer felt*.

My mind plays along with the universe and its cruel joke, saying, *This is what you don't have. This is what you should have.* And then there are the comments in the playground, about how my life is 'easier' because I 'only' have one child. They all mesh together to compound the grief that was felt each time a loss happened, as I stand on the oval waiting to pick up my solo child from school and other families pile their three-plus kids into their people movers. Their words expressed feel to me like they come with the undertone of me being less of a mother than them because I have fewer living children. I respond with little emotion, 'Yes I have one,' specifically not using the word 'just'. What I really want to do is scream out and let them know WHY I have one child. Tell them about the loss of three bodies and three souls that didn't make it earthside. About the agony and heartbreak of each loss, the secrecy of each experience hidden from friends, family, from the world because it was a taboo topic, deemed a failure from society, when I don't feel that way at all. Each loss completely different than the others.

I have wanted to be a mother since I can remember. I had wanted the wedding, the marriage with a best friend and then to breed and create the nuclear family I was brought up in, seemingly perfect. Those things happened for me, after a few false starts, and within twelve months of marriage we were pregnant! One Sunday, when I was about twelve weeks pregnant, we told a group of friends who were completely elated and thrilled for us. Finally ... finally, it was our turn. The next day, I got the worst phone call I'd received since the endless calls with bad news I'd had regarding my parents, who also died within the period of time when these losses happened.

'Your baby is 80% likely to have Down's syndrome.' That statement had me almost collapsing to the floor of an inner suburban coffee shop. Yet, somehow, I paid for my coffee, gathered my work belongs and got to my car, where I hysterically called my husband. The next day we did the amniocentesis (a test to remove amniotic fluid and test for common genetic conditions). Afterwards we were told it was 99% likely that our first son's fate was DS. I prayed, I bargained with the universe, with God, that that 1% chance would hold true and he would be genetically 'normal'. My husband said he took one look at the screen and simply knew our son did have this one in 100 genetic condition. The wait the next day was the longest of my life, longer than the day my dad went in for surgery for bowel cancer and finally came out, fighting on for five years before losing his epic battle. Longer than the day my mother waited for the medical appointment that would confirm she had the horrid neurological condition Parkinson's disease, which led to an agonising mental and physical demise for eleven years. Both diagnoses happening within the same month and the subsequent seemingly never-ending health battles, when I was just twenty-six years old. Their illnesses and deaths happened way before I could even ask my parents what I was like as a baby or compare this to my unborn children as babies, or imagine how my parents could be a positive part of my unborn children's lives as grandparents.

On this particular day, waiting, each agonising second of the day was filled with another bargain to God or the universe, asking that our son didn't have this genetic disease which could mean a difficult life ahead. At 5pm, the call came: 'Your baby does have Down's syndrome. I can do the D&C tomorrow at 7am.' The unjustness of my first pregnancy, at thirty-six years old unfolding in this way, the trauma of having no time to decide his fate with reason, no counselling, no information about the severity of his genetic disease. Only an assumption of what our decision would be and an enforced time line of which I would no longer be carrying him. The way it unfolded without compassion, thought or consideration for my son from professionals left me suicidal because of the hormones that were circulating in my still-pregnant body and the intense agony, grief and emotion they bought with them.

The lasting effect is only coming to its full force now, with a recently suggested PTSD diagnosis 8.5 years on. Yet, it truly feels like that phone call and the traumatic sequence of events that unfolded in the following twenty-four hours was only yesterday.

Falling pregnant again ten months later was the greatest thing that has ever happened to me, but to add to the long list of grief, my mother finally completed her degenerative demise from the cruellest of illnesses, physically and emotionally, when I was thirteen weeks pregnant with my living son.

With my husband's parents both also having passed, my son had no grandparents, and we would raise a child without the guidance of family. We agreed we must give him a sibling, we couldn't repeat the history of my mother's life who was an 'only child' and *despised it,* as she reported to me when I was a child. However, the losses of my final two babies, this time both girls, is a blur. It's a blur of dates and how many weeks along I was. The bottom line is, they didn't make it. I was now going to live with the same family dynamic my mother had lived throughout her life – my son would be an only child. But really the bottom line, the saving grace, the good in all of this agony, heartbreak and trauma, is that the child who did make it is a truly old soul. Perhaps his soul did resemble our first son in some way, but this time we were graced with a healthy, robust body that stayed too.

Working with other families is a constant reminder of what we don't have and what we have lost. It has been filled with jealousy, heartbreak and intolerance, but has provided an opportunity to work on my own trauma which is an ongoing journey of acceptance of having one child, and not the family I had imagined. I always thought I would have up to four living children and my parents would by my side to support me emotionally and physically. However, I am filled with gratitude for my son and husband. We have raised him independently without emotional or daily logistical help from anyone and he is a true gift. We have bonded as a united front and raised him without the negative trademarks of what an 'only child' is accordingly to society. He's not spoilt and he's not shy, by any stretch. He is self-assured, confident, intelligent, wise beyond his years, thoughtful and an incredibly social boy. He embodies my parents, what they left with me to pass onto him, what they would have wanted all my children to have, all wrapped up in one precious thriving body and soul.

SELF-RELIANCE AND PERSEVERANCE WHEN YOU'RE ALL YOU HAVE

My mother used to say, 'No-one cares about anyone but themselves, Georgina.' My mother was very maternal and resilient and instilled in my brother and me strong family values. However, she lacked insight into her own faults and also thrived on criticism, ego and a facade of perfectionism. The notion of having to rely on yourself rather than anyone else for success or happiness may not be as cold-hearted as she described, as this gem has held truth for me. It has rung true, as without my parents, with no grandparents, cousins, aunts or uncles and only a brother, it really has been up to me to find the happiness I deserve, alongside my husband who truly supports me and my business which drives and fulfils me every single day. My dad was the hardest worker (apart from my husband) I have ever known. He was a mover and shaker in every community of which he was part of. He made shit happen! He never took no for an answer, whether he was campaigning for a cause in local government or his own business. Assertive, kind, loyal to a fault and with a wicked sense of humour, he didn't rely on family for support. I guess he didn't have any family either; his parents had passed away, his elder brother died in WWII, his sister, although alive, until recently lived interstate, and his first four children were fairly absent in his life once he met my mum and had my brother and me. This left my mum, brother and me to be a united front, as our parents raised us with high standards, old-school values and beliefs. Dad had to provide for us when blow after financial blow kept coming, whether it was the recession in 1994 or the stint with a scammer (not a common occurrence in the

1990s), he continually had to rebuild his business, his resilience and depend on himself to build something from nothing again and again. Just like my dad, I have reinvented myself again and again. When you don't find the career that fulfils you or the career your university degree is supposed to provide, society can see you as a failure. I have attained three university degrees (that's 11.5 years consecutively at university if you are wondering!); I just never found my calling. Until the past few years when all the skills, experience and lessons learnt have combined to create my 'dream career'. Though some may call that failure, it's an excessive amount of life experience, both personally and professionally, that gives me the maturity, empathy, understanding and compassion for the families I work with who are in some of the darkest periods of their lives. This is the preservice passed onto me from my dad. I will not stop until it is done. I will not stop until I achieve what I am called to do. I may need help along the way and divert to another path occasionally, but I will not stop achieving and reaching the goals of this business, what I personally want to achieve and the message I want to spread to parents of babies and toddlers. My parents (despite their faults, of which there were many) were my greatest teachers, and their perseverance and self-reliance I live out today in business and in life.

COMPARISON: THE THIEF OF JOY – NAVIGATING AUTHENTICITY IN BUSINESS

I believe Brené Brown was right when she said, 'Comparison is the thief of joy.' Even the strongest, most secure women can go down the rabbit hole of seeing the glistening stories on social media with their filters and flattering angles and compare themselves to these false facades.

Physically, many women alter their appearance so they can look better and believe they will 'feel better inside'. They have plastic surgery to enhance themselves or take something away that society's messaging tells them is genetically flawed. In my business, I have done this ... repeatedly.

A slave to the follower numbers on competitors' Instagram pages or other businesswomen I admire, I follow along and check what seems like ever-growing numbers regularly. Following these businesswomen from Instagram to their website and analysing their websites to see if I can find the WHY of their success, and why they are more successful than me – which, of course, is ultimately only measured by the amount of followers, nothing more.

Two years ago, on one of these rabbit holes, which journeyed me to a competitor's Instagram profile, I pinned her success to a course and thought, *What a great idea! Yes, I should do that too!* Even though our ethos and how we approach our work is like night and day, I still thought it seemed like a great (random) idea. And so that's what I did.

I spent weeks creating a course, the videos and written content. I uploaded it on my website, talked about it on my socials ... and ... crickets ... Not the sound of a metaphorical cash register, not a ding on my email alerts as Kajabi let me know of a buyer. Instead, silence. Well actually, I got one sale! One big whopping sale! I made between $200-300 for all those weeks of work because I randomly followed someone else and assumed that what worked for another business owner would work for me. I mean, it's not the worst business mistake I've made but it is the most inauthentic one.

Since then, I have adopted an authentic approach to the content, offers and products I put out into the world. I have a particular way of working. I like the way I work, it feels in alignment with my knowledge, who I am, my skills and my experiences in parenting and in loss, which give me maturity, empathy and wisdom, which is incredibly unique. Yes, I can be direct; I am straightforward (just like my father). I will tell you how it is, but I have softened that approach over the years for the sleep-deprived mummas I am dealing with. I also use a great amount of humour, mostly in a self-deprecating way, as well as being insanely empathetic. It's so important amongst the noise on social media that we stay true to ourselves, that we look at the stories and pictures we scroll through each day as entertainment, not as truth and definitely not as a yard stick for what we should do, who we should be and how we should work. We should be authentically us.

THE LONG GAME ...

When those that went before us as businesswomen said, *It's the long game* – they weren't joking! There are elements to business that need to be built, steadied and improved with failures, successes and lived experience.

It's so easy to look at 'success stories' and feel it has happened quickly for others. But if I look at my own journey, the last five years of business have changed in the professional landscape and vastly within my own business. The first website I had was a shocker! Clunky, not user friendly and SO hard to create. I built a new website and created a membership in the first eighteen months of my business. The podcast was created in 2022 and has taken me time to learn how to technically record it and then execute episodes on a regular basis. The referrals from other mothers have taken time, but now this is one of my main sources of business. There have been lives, podcast interviews on other podcasts, business groups joined (many of which were fruitless), talks in a community setting, trade shows, writing in this book, presenting masterclasses and the endless back-end work that is involved, including Facebook ads, creating brochures, presenting to my membership each week, answering messages in DMs late at night, responding to emails and learning everything to do with the website, email marketing, funnels, lead magnets and opt-ins. All the while consulting with clients! To think I couldn't do any of these five years ago and would run a mile to avoid all this necessary tech, marketing and back-end activities. Now, I do it all! If I can't do it, I find another professional who will help me, and we do it together.

It IS a long game. There aren't many overnight successes, but the growth from learning all these necessary elements for a business to run is astounding and insanely rewarding.

Georgina Windebank

G eorgina Windebank is a holistic sleep consultant, qualified naturopath and mother. Born on the Mornington Peninsula and living in Melbourne for many years, eighteen months ago, she and her husband made the country change to Albury/Wodonga to give their family a slower-paced life as their son started school. They took a leap of faith as they didn't know anyone in the area at all! Georgina's husband was working almost 24/7 (a business owner as well) and she and her son weren't seeing him very much while living the busy city life, hence the move to the country.

Georgina has travelled extensively (Asia, Europe, South America, New Zealand etc.), on her own, with friends, her husband and with their young son. She has several university degrees – Bachelor of Communication (Public Relations/Marketing), Graduate Certificate of Media Sales and Bachelor of Health Science (Naturopathy/Nutrition). Georgina has had many careers, each of them a stepping stone to finally discovering the rewarding and successful work she now does as a holistic sleep consultant. She wanted to stay home with her son as long as she could, so Georgina started her business in Melbourne lockdown as her 2.5-year-old son played at her feet.

Within her business, The Holistic Sleep Project, she incorporates her knowledge as a naturopath into her work as a holistic sleep consultant (Australia-wide and internationally). This creates a unique approach to solving sleep issues for families who are struggling in those first few years of parenthood.

Her podcast *The Holistic Baby and Toddler Sleep Podcast* is hugely popular amongst parents who have a holistic approach to their child's wellbeing. One element to the podcast is interviewing professionals who are leaders in their chosen fields and who also have a holistic approach to their work with babies, toddlers or the postpartum health of mothers. Georgina has an online membership which she started three years ago and several one-to-one sleep support packages, which completely transform the sleep of babies and toddlers (and their families). She runs regular masterclasses and shows up daily on Instagram to connect with her very loyal followers. She has a fantastic base of referrals and has created a beautiful online community. Georgina has created a life that works around school hours, has made a significant lifestyle move and created all the elements which are necessary for a successful business.

Apart from her unique approach to baby and toddler sleep challenges, it is the trauma and grief Georgina has had to overcome in the same field that she works in that makes her work so profound and unique.

Georgina has had to overcome powerful emotions such as grief, jealousy and sadness when working with babies, when she has lost three babies during pregnancy herself.

It has been very confronting and it would often result in feeling devastated at the end of some days, yet she would pick herself up and go back the next day and face it all again. Time has helped Georgina, talking about these topics of miscarriage, medical termination, pregnancy, fertility – topics that women deal with each day. Group counselling with other women who lost their pregnancies, individual counselling, being kind to and acknowledging herself for all she has overcome and built in this time despite this trauma has been therapeutic and enabled her to begin to deal with the trauma of her own situation so Georgina can continue to do the work she adores.

Self-belief in her business and capabilities, alongside the support of her husband, has all paid off. He has been particularly supportive of Georgina staying home when their son was little in lieu of any family support (both sets of parents have all passed away) as she built her business and stayed home with their son in the early years.

After so much searching, false starts and mistakes in her career, Georgina has finally found what she enjoys and it gets incredible results with the babies and toddlers she works with. She uses all the skills accumulated from other professions that have come together to create this vocation. The maturity she has developed from these life experiences and trauma is invaluable and served her in this role when communicating with emotional parents, showing professionalism and being empathetic.

QUALIFICATIONS
Bachelor of Health Science (Naturopathy), Adv Dip of Nutrition
Bachelor of Communication (Public Relations), Adv Dip Marketing
Graduate Certificate in Media Sales
Holistic Sleep Consultant (IMPI-USA)

Podcast: *The Holistic Baby and Toddler Sleep Podcast*
Website: theholisticsleepproject.com
Instagram: instagram.com/theholisticsleepproject

Weathering the Storms

Jewels Harrison

Fear and devastation gripped my heart and continued to seep into my soul ... why me? Why is it that I always seem to be facing huge storms, never getting a break, forever being knocked down, only to have to drag myself back up again? I tuned out once the doctor told me I had miscarried my baby three weeks after their twin. I didn't know what to think. My head was in a very dark cloud. This was now our fifth and sixth miscarriage. I didn't know how much more I could take. All the dreams I'd planned were no more. My joy has been snatched away ... again – holes left in my heart for each of them. It wasn't fair, life sucked. All I wanted to do was curl up in a ball and die. I felt like a failure; to my babies who I never had the chance to hold, who could never enjoy life and all it had to offer; to my husband who wanted children as much as I did. Little did I know, this wasn't going to be our last tragic loss.

You could never have prepared me for the life I was living; the devastation, numbness, doing life on autopilot. Experiencing such emotional highs, to have them shattered into a million pieces. I never imagined this would be my journey – to carry life and constantly have it snatched away.

After the first few losses, I stopped confiding, talking or even speaking out loud about it anymore. People always seemed to want to offer their advice on something they know nothing about. They would pity me or feel I was always negative. I didn't let them into the battlefield taking place in my mind on a daily basis. I felt no-one would understand or cope with the weight I was carrying. All I needed was someone to be there, to listen and give me a hug.

It took so much strength, determination and pure grit to fight through years of consistent storms. These cyclones of destruction constantly caused by body, mind, soul and emotions to feel weary, devastated, negative and heartbroken. My joy was robbed, my dreams crumbled, shadowed with despair and helplessness. There were constant tears (mostly silent and alone at night). I was weighed down with pure loneliness, feeling like a failure on many levels, incomplete, as if all hope was depleted. It was a dark stormy season for me physically, emotionally and verbally.

Many years (and a further four miscarriages) later, we discovered we were pregnant once again. At our morphology scan (twenty weeks), we were asked if we wanted to know what we were having, and of course we did. When we were told we were having a boy I burst into tears (happy tears). Approximately ten years previously, a few months after getting married, I had an extremely real dream. (I understand that many people may not believe in God, but for me this dream was extremely instrumental in my perseverance and resilience to continuing the journey of becoming a mother.) In my dream, I had a baby girl in my arms and was told by God that she was mine, but that I could only have her on 'loan' for the day. I held her, showered her with kisses, became lost in her gorgeous eyes, inhaled her smell and her entire essence, played with her tiny fingers, toes and feet. I couldn't take my eyes off her beautiful, pure face. The dream was so real that I woke with a jolt in bed, searching and scanning our dark room for our baby's cot. When asked by my husband, 'What happened, are you okay?' I desperately asked, 'Where's our baby girl? Tell me … we have a baby girl …' Confused, he said, 'No' – and I burst into tears, disappointed that the dream wasn't true, that I couldn't hold her again.

But it was this dream that I tucked away in my heart, as a promise that kept me hopeful, prayerful and crossing my fingers and toes for the next nine-plus years, as we endured ten tragic and devastating miscarriages. In the tough times, I reverted back to the dream, to the promise, to her beautiful face that I had etched into my mind and heart. I continued to believe I would have my baby girl … one day. So when the doctor told me we were having a boy – I cried happy tears and was overjoyed, knowing that in the future, I would be having another baby – my baby girl who I still held in my heart.

In life, our circumstances are often fuelled by our attitude, which stems from our life experience. Life itself and the choices we make in the tough times have an enormous impact on the way we see things, our position in society and who we become.

Life's tragedies can often leave scars which stay with us forever. Depending on how we look at those scars determines whether they cripple us for the rest of our lives or if they are a reminder of what we have been through and, more importantly, what we have overcome.

Over a period of nine years, suffering ten miscarriages, I had every excuse to shut myself off from the world. Words can never express what a woman/couple goes through after having a miscarriage. The wounds cut deep and the pain and memory stays with you forever. Time, as well as choosing to have a positive attitude, helped me move on and get better at dealing with the pain. It is a long and lonely road to travel, without any closure. No funeral or wake to grieve properly with close friends and relatives, just my doctor telling me, 'Rest, don't drive, don't lift anything. Take painkillers if required and you may have bleeding for up to a week.' It was extremely hard to have a good attitude, especially when I was reminded of my pain every time I saw someone pregnant, a mother with a pram at the shops, or worse still, when as a police officer, I had to help deliver a baby in the back of an ambulance, with a mother who was heavily under the influence of drugs. Life is not fair, but at the time, I knew I had to continue to believe in my dream. That one day, I would have a baby of my own.

Life has thrown many challenges my way and yet through perseverance and resilience developed over time, I was able to accomplish so much. I still face many challenges on a daily basis but I know to keep pushing forward towards my goals, regardless of how tired and weary I am. Pushing forward doesn't aways mean you have to keep moving. Sometimes, in order to move forward, you need to pause, take a breath, find your direction again and then continue with your journey.

After we took many pauses and breaths, we continued our journey towards our dream. In December 2011, after twenty-five hours of labour, I was rushed in for an emergency caesarean where our first miracle child was born. He was amazing in every way and I could not stop the feeling of pure joy. We hadn't made it through the storm yet though as I had major complications and Mark was left with our precious baby for four hours while I was in surgery fighting for my life. Even though the storm was big, I never lost focus on my dream.

In September 2013, my promised miracle baby girl was born. She was beautiful and pure, and my heart burst with happiness as soon as I saw her. She was even better than in my dreams.

A few years later in January 2017, our family was complete with another miracle baby boy. He was gorgeous and made me smile with such gratitude, appreciation and happiness.

My children are my happy place, each one a delight to my soul. Sometimes in life, it can take a long time (even years) to obtain our dreams, but once we do, the journey is always worth it. All the heartache, tears, hard work, sleepless nights, challenges … all worth it to embrace your dream.

HOW I WEATHER THE STORMS

Focus on the Goal: This is what gets me up in the morning, gives me purpose and is something I will always be passionate about. With my business, I have kept the first drawings and designs I made of my logo. This reminds me of how far I've come and of what to look forward to in the future. This also gives me clarity on *why I do what I do* and keeps me focused on what is important – helping others in need.

In my personal life, it was the dream I held onto that kept me focused. And when my baby girl was four weeks old, I took a photo of her, as her face was exactly the same as in my dream, even down to the way her lips slightly curled into a smile as she slept. I still have this photo visible today (alongside my sons), as a constant reminder that dreams do come true if you don't lose sight of your dream, and you are prepared to endure whatever it takes to achieve it.

Choose Your Attitude: One vital key in life is your attitude and how you perceive situations you're faced with. Often, it can be extremely hard to keep a good attitude due to how we are feeling at the time. When we are knocked off our feet, it depends where our head is at and what our thoughts, feelings and emotions are saying to us. You can feel weary, lonely, exhausted, trapped, depressed, stressed, anxious, heavy-hearted, broken and ready to give up … even curl up into a ball til the end of time.

Sometimes, we subconsciously focus on all the negatives in our situation and often (especially in a big storm) it can be ridiculously difficult to find the good. As an example, me trying to find three positives with having a miscarriage, when I was in the middle of utter despair. But with time and looking from a different perspective, I could thank God that

I'm still alive, that I miscarried early in the pregnancy and that I have had a husband to support me.

Prepare For the Storm: Know the weather forecast and prepare for it as much as possible. Like, do you need an umbrella and a warm jacket? A hat, sunglasses and sunscreen? Or to secure the whole house, get supplies, generators, something to communicate with? Some storms we can prepare for in life, and others we can't.

In business, there are storms we see coming. We can either avoid them or tackle them head-on with the knowledge of what's coming. Others we have no idea when or where the storm comes from or how much damage it will cause. We need to keep checking the weather forecast, keeping our finger on the pulse, so we can be prepared for the storms.

Do Not Ever Let Others Tell You It's Impossible … It's Only Impossible for Them:
I was told:

'If it's not happening, maybe you aren't meant to have kids.'

'You must have done something against God at some time for this to be happening to you.'

'You're not blessed if you don't have kids.' So much negativity!

It's hard to soar like an eagle (with your dream), when you are constantly being attacked by smaller birds (even those closest to you). Remember, people bring others down for different reasons; mainly jealousy, pain, hurt, their own low self-esteem or low self-confidence.

In the business world, when people see you have a great idea, they either want to steal it from you or tell you it's a bad idea. They tell you it will never succeed, just to deter you and make you falter and rattle your confidence. Alternatively, if they see you are doing well and gaining momentum, they may try to undermine or discredit you personally, especially on social media. Be confident in yourself and your dream. I once had a dream/idea about a girls' youth program, however, it was stolen from me and given to someone else to run. The program got off the ground but because it wasn't their dream, it was never successful and therefore failed.

Time Is Inevitable: We all face storms in life but what matters is how we deal with them. They range from cyclones that take away everything you hold dear, hailstorms causing intense damage, a deluge of nonstop pouring rain that last days/weeks and causes flooding and road closures, to a light rain that effects your outdoor plans for the day, or a sun-shower that can be refreshing, but also uncomfortable, as it becomes humid and dampens everything, so plans may need to be cancelled. Big or small, all storms can be weathered. There will always be a way through to the other side, when the sun will shine bright to warm us again. Storms only last a certain time; they cannot go on forever. All storms have an end. We may be left with bruises, scars or our whole life turned upside-down, however, it is in these moments that our true strength, character and determination shines through.

SOME THOUGHTS TO REMEMBER

- Life is hard, but keep focused on the goal.
- Have a good attitude to life, family, friends and your business.
- At times it can be a lonely road – you need to be your own cheer-leader – this is what builds character.
- Prepare for the storms. This will save you a whole lot of time/pain, which may be crucial to your success.
- Remain positive. Lead by example and only if you have to … use words.
- Be authentic, transparent and confident in who you are.
- Never become what you think others want you to be.
- Do the little things well – this will give you confidence to tackle the

bigger things you didn't think were possible.

- When you are tested in the storms, find your inner strength – trust me, it's there.
- Know your strengths and weaknesses. If you need to, ask for help.
- Always appreciate and be grateful to others for what they do for you.

Together, my husband and I have weathered many storms and challenges head-on during our twenty-one years of marriage. Some of these storms we saw coming, so we were prepared for them, but others hit us without warning, knocking us over. Mark's support has encouraged me to be the best version of myself that I can be, and despite all the storms, we are still standing. Hopefully my journey so far will inspire others who may be on their own challenging journey and need to feel they can still accomplish their goals in life, whilst weathering the storms … as I believe I've learnt the art of dancing in the rain.

Jewels Harrison

J ewels is an extraordinary woman in every way. She is completely self-less, passionate, loves unconditionally, Tonka Tough and always goes the extra mile to help those in need.

From a young age Jewels loved sports especially swimming, where she won state titles and competed in the Australian Championships. Jewels loved to babysit and volunteered teaching swimming lessons and Sunday school. Her desire intensified when she witnessed so many kids neglected, abused, bullied and with mental health issues. Jewels volunteered copious amounts of hours to her local youth group where she built rapport and trust mentoring young people and responding to calls all hours of the night to those self-harming. Her passion landed her at a youth centre coordinating youth camps for up to nine hundred students. Jewels was in her element. This was where she met her husband Mark and they have been married for twenty-one years.

Jewels spoke to Members of Parliament at a leadership forum in Canberra about issues young people face and strategies to make things better. Jewels was invited to be a part of a young women in leadership group run by her local MP. Jewels became PA to the director of a college before becoming a lifeguard/swim coach while her and her husband trained to become NSW police officers. For ten years she worked in three of the busiest and roughest stations in Western Sydney and experienced things that still haunt her even after she was medically discharged.

Jewels heart's desire and dream was to become a mother. Little did she know that she would need every ounce of strength and resilience for this to come to pass. After ten miscarriages, multiple curettes, operations on her womb, over 1,200 clexane injections, hundreds of blood tests and specialist visits, Jewels and Mark finally celebrated having three miraculous, beautiful children. This was not without complications and all were diagnosed with autism at an early age.

Raising three autistic children is extremely challenging but also rewarding. With her experience and personal insight after recently discovering she too has autism gave her an even deeper understanding into how her children think, act and why they have meltdowns.

While maintaining this extremely high-demanding lifestyle, Jewels created and designed the *Unique StarShine App* which launched end of 2022. The app helps organise reports, documents and communication for someone with a disability or special need. Jewels realised how enormous the need was to organise all her children's documents and communication needed with specialists, doctors, NDIS, education departments, agencies and support workers.

Recently, Jewels and Mark have started homeschooling their autistic children. By orchestrating and creating a loving, encouraging and safer environment this has brought the family so much closer. Jewels often says, 'My children are my world … they are my heartbeat behind everything that I do,' and her life is a testimony of this.

What Jewels has accomplished in her life is extraordinary. She has endured all that life has thrown at her yet still has the capacity to give to the community whilst juggling her unique family and lifestyle – TRULY INSPIRING!

BUSINESS ACHIEVEMENTS

Entrepreneur

Founder/CEO of Unique StarShine Pty Ltd

Inspirational Speaker

AusMumpreneur 2023 – Gold Award for Digital Innovation/Tech

AusMumpreneur 2023 – Finalist for Disabled Business Excellence

Cape Ability Network Business Awards 2023 – Second Place for Business Award

Cape Ability Network Business Awards 2023 – Finalist for Product Award

Women Changing The World Awards 2024 – Finalist for Innovation Award

Women Changing The World Awards 2024 – Bronze Award winner in Science, Tech & Engineering

AusMumpreneur 2024 - Finalist in the following six categories:

- Creative Entrepreneur
- Digital Innovation
- Digital Service
- Disabled Business Excellence
- Overcoming The Odds
- Product Innovation

Author

Website: uniquestarshine.com

Facebook: facebook.com/uniquestarshine

Instagram: instagram.com/unique_starshine

LinkedIn: linkedin.com/in/jewels-harrison-unique-starshine

Igniting My Fire

My Path to Purpose and Passion

Joanne Caruso

Many of us go through life wondering what our purpose is. I've always had a feeling that my purpose was bigger than me and that I am here on this Earth to make a difference, in whatever it was I would end up doing. I didn't know exactly what that purpose was, but I knew one day it would find me.

Discovering my passion was more of a puzzle. I invested a lot of time and money in learning new things, as I really didn't know what my passion was or how to find it. And still today, I find myself consistently trying new things, as I never know when I will find something else that will ignite a new spark.

Sometimes we know we want to make changes to our life or career, in order to discover our purpose and passion, but the 'WHAT TO DO?' is always the million-dollar question. Sometimes, however, events happen that force us to make changes.

When someone gets married, they don't have divorce on their mind. But after eleven years of marriage, I found myself divorced at thirty-five, with three young daughters aged three, five and seven to support.

Back then, there was no such thing as 'flexible working arrangements'

– well, not where I was working. So, after being a stay-at-home mum for over five years, I returned to the paid workforce as a full-time employee.

Before my maternity leave, I had worked for two Melbourne newspapers in the HR department; a career I started at seventeen, straight out of high school. It wasn't a career I chose, as I actually wanted to join the police force. I continued my studies with evening classes twice a week to gain the qualifications I felt I needed for my career, three years at TAFE and then university.

After my first daughter was born, I went back to work full-time, and shortly after, I was pregnant again with my second daughter. I remember leaving for work one day, heavily pregnant, coming out of the driveway, slamming on the brakes and thinking, *I can't do this anymore*. Resigning was an easy decision because having two daughters twenty-three months apart and trying to hold down a career was tough. Twenty months later, my third daughter arrived.

Being a stay-at-home mum had its challenges too. As a mother, I questioned if I was 'maternal enough' because how I was with my children looked totally different to how my own mother was with me. My mother was raised to be and accepted her role as a stay-at-home wife and mother, whereas I was given different opportunities and wanted both a family and a career.

I found housework boring and unfulfilling and I yearned for adult conversation. There were many times I wished my sisters had children, so we could share advice and find common ground – just like what I saw with my parents and aunts and uncles and the dozens of cousins I grew up with. For much of this period in my life, I felt lonely and found this to be an emotionally challenging time. I didn't know where I belonged. I felt my whole identity had disappeared and that an imposter had taken over. Who was I? Who had I become?

Financially, money was tight – we were now a family of five living on one income with a mortgage, and I missed working outside of the home. I decided to study a certificate in accounting at TAFE, as my sister, who was an accountant, had offered me some casual work. This gave me some of the adult conversation I craved, and I felt I was contributing to the household budget.

My marriage collapsed when my youngest was three years old, and with three young daughters to support, I became the sole provider for my family. I was determined for my daughters not to 'miss out' on anything, despite being a single mum, so the decision to return to full-time work was the path I chose.

I returned to HR because that was what I knew. For the next fifteen years, I worked in a variety of industries. I did contracts, worked full-time, part-time and anything in-between. I was never without work but there was a void in my heart. The passion for HR was long gone.

At forty, I attempted to change careers and I studied a diploma in beauty therapy part-time while also working part-time. Once the course was completed, I landed my dream HR role, so beauty took the back seat. The role took me travelling, which I loved, to Singapore, Malaysia and regularly interstate, but after three years of being away from home at least once a month, it had taken its toll on my family, so I resigned and did contract work until I could work out what I wanted to do.

Human psychology has always fascinated me, so I decided to do an intensive transformational coaching course that dug deep into the human psyche and the 'why' we behave the way we do. It was a worthwhile course and taught me so much about myself too. Learning about transformational coaching was a good segue to how the brain works and how we are able to heal ourselves through thought, and an intensive three-day workshop I attended with Dr Joe Dispenza covered all that in more detail. To tap into my own healing abilities, I also studied reiki as well as a plethora of other short course and workshops.

I rented a room to see clients for massage and facials as I really enjoyed those aspects from my beauty diploma. I did some further training to learn about skin care products and started making my own chemical-free vegan skin care to use on my clients and to sell at markets.

I was working in HR part-time and going to markets most weekends. I loved market life; the comradery of meeting other stall holders and dealing directly with customers was rewarding.

There was plenty of growth for me during those fifteen years, and as you can probably tell, I spent a lot of time trying new things and moving forward. I also learnt a great deal about myself and my life.

Here are some of my major take-aways from that time:

BOUNDARIES AND FEELING OBLIGATED

Being a working mother, especially a *single* working mother, I found myself being pulled in every direction. As well as having the stress of providing for my family – I never wanted my daughters to miss out just because 'I was divorced' so I found it hard to say no to them – I had an ex-husband to contend with and that wasn't always easy. I was working full-time hours in a stressful career that didn't allow for flexible working arrangements, and to top it off, if my daughters misbehaved or didn't listen to my parents, I would have my parents to deal with too!

Looking back, I wasn't very good at setting boundaries, and I accepted certain situations. I now realise some of the stressful times I experienced could have been avoided.

I felt obligated to my parents because I needed their help. Instead of finding a job that allowed for flexible working arrangements, I tolerated it because I didn't want to appear weak or unreliable. I didn't want to rock the boat.

GUILT

As a working mother, I often felt guilt; the guilt of coming home frustrated, exhausted and grumpy from a busy workday, leaving little time to be a fun mother to my daughters. I struggled to switch off and relax and found myself regularly in fight or flight mode. This took its toll on my health and wellbeing, and I started gaining weight, holding on to that negative emotion of guilt and stress and finding comfort in snacking!

VULNERABILITY

I felt I needed to be a strong role model to my daughters – *all the time*, often playing the role of both mother and father. There were many times where I was so exhausted or felt defeated that I would look forward to bedtime, just so I could have a big cry and no-one would see me. Being vulnerable was hard for me because I saw vulnerability as a weakness and failure.

STAYING AUTHENTIC

People will have a perception of who they think you are rather than who you *truly* are. As you evolve, being true to *you* and staying authentic is important. I often hear people say they just smile, and no-one knows what's going on behind that smile. When you are true to yourself, you no longer need to hide behind an inauthentic facade and life becomes so much easier.

DON'T WAIT UNTIL DEATH KNOCKS AT THE DOOR TO MAKE CHANGES TO YOUR LIFE. MAKE THEM NOW

My father passed away suddenly, which was a big shock to me. For some reason, I never thought of life without him, and his passing hit me hard. I was his tomboy growing up, and I spent much of my time outside helping him fix things. He taught me everything I know about power tools, and he gave me the confidence to do things for myself.

Sixteen months later, my eldest sister passed away from cancer, at age fifty-four. That hit me harder. I always saw my sister as my protector, my confidante because she was always there for me. Sure, we had our ups and downs as sisters do, but in the latter part of her life, our bond grew stronger and I miss her immensely.

My sister was the reason I got into colonics. I remember the first time she had her appointment, she called me on her way home and told me all about it and, sure enough, I booked in for an appointment because she told me I would love it! She was right. The seed was planted that day.

Something happens when someone close passes away. Sure, it is a massive wake-up call to make positive changes to your life as it can all be over in a split second, but it's almost like all the drama of life no longer matters; the priorities have changed and the only thing that does matter is finding peace within and being grateful for our loved ones that are still with us. Nothing prepares you for grief and there is no time limit on how long you grieve. It's about getting used to a different type of living. You are no longer just living your life; you are living the life of your passed loved ones as well.

By the time I decided that colonics was the career change I had been yearning for, I knew it had been the missing link to my WHAT TO DO. So, I picked up the books again and studied colonics – not just one colonics course but two!

There is so much more to colonics than just the poop. It's about making the mind-body connection and letting go of trauma and negative emotion. It's about hydration, nourishment and healing, nurturing the body, the mind and the spirit.

I didn't know back then, but every single course I've done, and the skills I've learnt, are all transferable to what I'm doing today. It took me years to figure it out, but without even knowing it, everything I had learnt over the years was all leading to my colonics and wellness centre.

Once qualified as a colonics hydrotherapist, I worked at a clinic during the evenings (after working during the day in HR) and on Saturdays. After working two jobs, six days a week, I finally left HR for good and picked up extra shifts at the clinic where I stayed until I opened my own company.

I have now completed my first year of my business and, I must say, I love every minute of it! I can't remember the last time I didn't jump out of bed in the morning, excited to go to work! I can now relate when people say, *If you love what you do, you never work another day in your life,* because that's exactly what this feels like. I love everything about what I do from meeting new clients to hearing their stories, to watching their transformations and improvements to their health and wellbeing. I have met some amazing people and I am so grateful that they have taken me along with them as they get their health back on track.

If you want something bad enough, your heart will take you there and you will achieve it. You just need to do the work and have trust in yourself that you can do it, no matter how old you are.

If you've been thinking of starting your own business, here are my top tips and hints to make that happen:

- Always do something towards your business, even if you don't know what it is.
  - When the children go to bed, it's a great time to work on your business.
  - Read a book or research.
  - Jot down ideas. Even if the ideas appear to be far-fetched, write them down as, you never know, they may make sense later.
- Start thinking of a business name and start designing your logo, business cards, flyers etc.

- Go to business workshops, seminars and events – your local council has a lot of free business events you can tap into to inspire you to move forward.
- Keep your plans and ideas to yourself – when you're excited about something, you want to tell everyone and share your exciting news. Until you're 100% sure on what you want to do, keep your plans and ideas to yourself and that way, you avoid any negative comments that will leave you doubting yourself.

Almost everything we learn along the way is transferrable in one way or another, so never see learning something new as a waste of time. Here is how my skill set has transferred to my business:

- Beauty therapy – massage techniques taught are used on my clients during the abdominal massage.
- Skin care – knowing which essential oils to use on my clients and which to avoid.
- Transformational coaching – every colonic treatment is a coaching session where my clients are being vulnerable and open up.
- Accounting certificate – it's important to know my numbers.
- HR qualifications – people management, policy and processes.

AND FINALLY, YOU'RE NEVER TOO OLD TO FOLLOW YOUR DREAM

When you look back through history, many famous women had success in their later years such as Julia Childs, Martha Stewart and J K Rowling, to name a few. You're never too old to chase your dreams and you're just as special and important as the next person, so what are you waiting for?

If you have determination, drive and, of course, passion, you will do well in whatever you decide you want to do. Just remember to TRUST and BACK yourself. If you trust and back yourself, then everyone else will too!

Joanne Caruso

Joanne Caruso is a proud mother to three adult daughters. She is a colonics hydrotherapist and the founder of Joanne's Temple Colonics & Wellness Centre, in Melbourne, Australia.

At the age of fifty-one, Joanne made a courageous decision to change careers and study colonics, as she had seen the benefits first-hand when her sister, Josephine, used colonics as part of her alternative cancer treatment to remove toxins from her body.

Understanding the mind-body connection, Joanne knows the importance of releasing negative emotions such as fear, anger, grief, guilt, stress and the effects these emotions have on our overall wellbeing. 'We tend to *hold on* to these emotions which remain stuck until we get to the point of being ready to let go.'

After spending over thirty years in the corporate world, Joanne opened Joanne's Temple Colonics & Wellness Centre in Melbourne's northern suburbs. Her mission is to create a space where people can come to heal, to be supported, to learn about themselves and to grow into their best authentic versions of who they are meant to be. Joanne is proud of her achievements; where many of her friends are preparing for retirement, Joanne's new career is just taking off.

Joanne provides a safe environment where her clients can open up and talk – if they want to – and work on releasing those blocked emotions. Whether you chat or sit quietly during your time with Joanne, you are her priority and her aim is to assist you to achieve your wellness goals.

Joanne is extremely proud of her daughters and seeing them achieve their own goals is rewarding.

Outside of work you will find her cooking, catching up with friends, tending to her vegetable garden, travelling and her never-ending home renovations. She has a thirst for knowledge and continues to study new things, with a short course or two always on the go. She has certifications in traditional colon hydrotherapy, Rojas technique colon hydrotherapy, diplomas in human resources, accounting and beauty therapy, along with many (many) other certifications including reiki and transformational coaching.

Website: joannestemplecolonics.com.au
Facebook: facebook.com/JoannesTempleColonics
Instagram: instagram.com/joannestemplecolonics/
LinkedIn: linkedin.com/in/joanne-caruso-b8a283a/

Embrace the Chaos

Jorja Wallace

'What is food to one, is to others bitter poison.'
– Roman philosopher Lucretius

At the risk of sounding nihilistic, I do not subscribe to the notion that there is a meaning to life. That there is a reason why we are here. That we need to find our purpose for being and then spend our life in servitude of that purpose. I have searched for a purpose because I thought that was what I was 'supposed' to do, but I have never truly believed one existed.

We are born, we live, we die. For the most part, life is a chaotic mess outside of our control. Sometimes it is beautiful, sometimes it is irrational, sometimes it is cruel. But I have found no joy in searching for a purpose.

In fact, focusing on purpose has caused quite the opposite; leading to what can only be described as an existential crisis spanning two-thirds of my life, bookended by losses that had a profound impact. A touch over two decades of feeling lost and confused, as if I missed some vital lesson in early schooling where everyone was given a handbook on how to be a human.

I always struggled with the '*what do you want to be when you grow up?'* question. I wanted to be and do so many things. Why did I have to choose just one, and then define myself around that choice? I was, and still am, passionate about so many things. I want to experience them all and be defined by none of them.

Even my attempts to define a purpose were flawed. I recently cleaned out my childhood bedroom, only to find a visual folio I had created for the transition from primary to high school. Under the heading *Future Ambitions,* I wrote *Please my mum and dad.* I cried for twelve-year-old me who had defined their worthiness by reference to the opinion of their parents. But, in retrospect, I know how the mindset of that little girl came to be.

The eldest child and eldest daughter to dairy farmers in rural north-east Victoria, conditions were right for the 'good girl persona' to come to pass. I was hardworking, eager to please and took seriously any responsibilities placed on my shoulders. With three younger siblings, and a flock of younger cousins (but for one), the adults would regularly ask me to 'look after' or 'entertain' the kids. In response, I would come up with games and activities, and position myself as a pseudo-parent, to which most, if not all, of my cousins and siblings would describe me as bossy.

I was nine years old when the colour of the world changed.

Between breaking out in an incurable inflammatory skin condition, and watching my uncle deteriorate from and eventually succumb to brain cancer, I started to search for reasons why these things were happening. The owner of a fairly literal brain, I couldn't understand how the expression 'everything happens for a reason' could possibly be true. What reason could there be for cancer? What reason could there be for my body to suddenly become alien and ugly?

1999 was the year things no longer made sense; it was also the moment I started to hate my body, rolling into the image-focused 2000s perfectly primed for my teenage years to be spent seeking external validation of my self-worth, through numerical grades on assignments, at the bottom of a bottle, or in the arms or bed of another. A hole that became darker the deeper I went into it, and had no good answers to my search for a purpose (and came close to ending unanswered in 2007).

Outwardly, I tried to keep up the 'good girl' persona, focusing on school and getting good grades, securing paid employment from the moment I was able to, and involving myself in any available extracurricular activities or leadership roles. I was told my talents lay in writing and 'arguing' (due to an obsession with justice), so I chose to study law and journalism at university, moving interstate to start the search for purpose yet again. Spoiler alert: I didn't find it, and, after September 2012, I could no longer bring myself to look for one.

'Life, at best, is bittersweet.' – Jack Kirby

Aligning more with the philosophy of absurdism, to me, 'purpose' is something humans create to justify our existence, whereas passions are the things that make us feel alive and able to immerse ourselves in every second life gives us. And I use the plural intentionally here, as I don't believe passion is a static concept, or that we get to have just one.

I have always been drawn to creative and expressive pursuits, finding that I feel most alive when I am using my hands to bring an idea to life. I have also loved seeking out information, operating in fact and solving puzzles, feeling a sense of euphoria when I can find an answer or a workable solution. And, as much as I find it difficult to connect with people, I truly find human behaviour fascinating, and I adore helping others to shine.

I prefer to have many fires burning, feeding them simultaneously and allowing the ones that no longer bring me warmth to slowly burn out.

A walking contradiction when it comes to doing things I love, what

I pursue in parallel must be deeply confusing to those who are unable to categorically place me into a predetermined societal box. But we are not bound to a singular time line for our life. There are many paths to take, many lives to live, and you can change yourself, and the course of your life, at any point in time.

And, sometimes, the course of life is changed for us.

In September 2012, I was finishing up a stint as the publications director for the university's weekly student magazine. It was my final trimester of university, and I had no idea what I wanted to do with my degrees when I graduated. I was leaning more to the field of journalism because I had loved my time in the editor's seat.

But that changed when my friend Bonnie suddenly and unexpectedly passed away.

An incredibly traumatic event for a twenty-two-year-old, made worse by being left to make death notifications to mutual friends, and then reading the media coverage that seemed to blanket the news cycle.

2012 was the year that the Mayan calendar had predicted the world would end. I was a member of the university student association, and we had, some weeks prior, held a meeting to discuss the theme for the upcoming student pub crawl. I had suggested we play off the 'end of the world' theme and do a 'zombie apocalypse' theme.

When the day for pub crawl came, members of the student association were, as usual, split between the two groups of student attendees. I was on the earlier crawl as a student chaperone, and Bonnie was on the later crawl as an attendee. We were going to meet at the final stop, but, for a number of reasons, Bonnie left her crawl early and went home.

At some point later that evening, or early the next day, Bonnie passed away. Although I have never been made aware of the exact cause, I know it was not as a direct result of that pub crawl. However, the media weren't going to let that get in the way of a 'good story'. Within days, a local newspaper had published a front-page story with a photo of Bonnie and the headline *The Day Bonnie's World Ended*, attributing her death to the student association-run pub crawl.

I recall seeing the newspaper and feeling like I had been punched. Still reeling from the death of a friend, and trying to reconcile what had happened, it was suddenly very easy to start telling myself that I had played a part. After all, I was on the student association, on the pub crawl, and I was the one who had come up with the theme.

If I can point to a time in my life of extreme vulnerability, this would be it. Some mutual friends deferred the semester, others left for weeks to process the loss, but I was the poor country kid on a partial scholarship (and massive FEE-HELP debt) – I could not afford to not finish the semester. I was interstate from family, and although my mum came up for a short period, I had to pull myself together and make it through to December. And I did, courtesy of a lot of alcohol and, at times, stupid, reckless, destructive behaviour.

This became the start of a long period in my life where I felt as if I was stuck in a state of freeze; going through the motions of life as the shell of the person I previously was, merely existing, not living, and not always making the healthiest of choices.

'In the midst of winter, I finally learned that there was in me an invincible summer.' – Albert Camus

When I reached down into the water in late December 2019 and pulled my baby up to my chest, everything I thought I was up to that point shattered. When they locked eyes with me and squeezed their tiny hand around my finger, it felt like time stood still. It was as if a mirror had been held up to me, and everything I had left unresolved came piling in.

What they don't tell you about having a newborn amid the world shutting down, is that there is A LOT of time spent sitting with your thoughts. Enter all the demons I had been running from. So, after a period of deep introspection, 2021 became the year I decided to give into the absurdity of life, and truly begin to savour the taste. It was the year I felt like life chewed me up and spat me back out in a form more beautiful and stronger than before.

In truth, there were three key moments in 2021 that became the foundation for change and acceptance of *what is*.

THE FOUNDATION

The year had started off poorly. The career I had been building over seven years seemed to be a casualty of motherhood. Naively, I had assumed any barriers to entry after maternity leave would be limited to mindset and maternal desire. I didn't expect to be let down by the same public service institution that had bestowed an award on me just over a year prior.

After being cast aside, I reached out to a former colleague and secured a secondment to another agency. Things hadn't gone to plan but, hey, it was a paid role and gave me the opportunity to relieve tension in my marriage and start to rebuild confidence (and my career).

What I didn't realise is that this experience planted the seeds of dissent. The fire that once kept me warm was now threatening to consume me.

THE PERSPECTIVE

A shift in mindset that had started to flicker when I became a mother in 2019 ignited into a full-blown flame. 2021 was a year of loss, grief, fear, uncertainty, pain, isolation and loneliness; with the most intense of those experiences crammed into August to September.

Fear and uncertainty when we entered Canberra's first (and only) pandemic lockdown in isolation after our toddler's former child care centre was named a potential exposure location. Exhaustion, isolation and loneliness throughout the lockdown period, juggling working from home and full-time child caring responsibilities, while my partner was classified an 'essential worker'.

Loss, grief and loneliness when a close childhood friend, Laura, passed away interstate from a long battle with an awful illness. Grief and loneliness when I silently observed the nine-year anniversary of Bonnie's death a few weeks later. And finally, fear, uncertainty and pain when I walked out of a vaccination appointment into the arms of a heart condition.

I learned of Laura's brain cancer diagnosis less than a year after Bonnie passed away, but I hadn't fully accepted or processed it. When she came to see me after her diagnosis in 2013, she named two songs and said she wanted them played at her funeral. After she left, I watched the music video for one on repeat for weeks, crying as I tried to process that I would lose another friend at some future unknown point in time, that each time I saw her could be the last.

February 2021 was the last in-person contact we had. We spent hours together in glorious sunshine listening to live music, and I watched her dancing and singing ecstatically to John Butler. We had one of our classic D&M (deep and meaningful) conversations to the sound of a band neither of us had heard before. There was a moment in time as their music played where I looked at her with such love and appreciation, and 'Carry You' by The Teskey Brothers has now become one of the songs I choose to remember her to, replacing the funeral song she had played me years earlier.

I was devastated when she passed in August 2021. But, unlike Bonnie, I had an opportunity to send Laura a message to tell her how much she meant to me and the impact she had had on my life. A rare opportunity I will forever be grateful for.

Laura gave me the gift of perspective – don't wait; the right time to live freely, boldly and courageously is right now.

THE IMPETUS

By the end of September 2021, I was broken and had completely lost my passion and zest for life. I was a shell of a human thanks to my health, predominantly confined to the couch, and, at best, a present in body but absent in mind mother.

Then, in November, when I was sure death was lurking behind one of the five thousand extra beats my heart was pounding out daily, I found the strength to embrace the absurdity of life and give in to *what is*. Instead of focusing on what hadn't gone to plan, and trying to 'find myself', I decided to start 'living' again through the pursuit of passions.

At this point, I didn't know what I liked anymore. I decided to take a huge risk and see if that led to any fires. I left my public service career behind and entered the world of small business.

'The only way to deal with an unfree world is to become so absolutely free that your very existence is an act of rebellion.' – Albert Camus

My business is not my purpose, because I do not believe I have one.

My business is a passion; for now. And when it no longer sets me alight or brings me warmth, I will search for another fire.

I am choosing to lean into the chaos and absurdity of life – I have no idea where it will take me, but I am here for it.

Jorja Wallace

Jorja is both a work in progress and a masterpiece. Described by those around her as passionate, courageous, resilient, authentic, determined, creative, bold and dynamic, Jorja is reinventing herself in her thirties after a long season of winter.

An award-winning small business owner, Jorja believes in leaving a room better than you found it and pursuing the things that set your soul on fire.

Hailing from a dairy farm in rural north-east Victoria, Jorja is currently based in Canberra, ACT, with her young child and husband. She studied a bachelor of laws and a bachelor of journalism at Bond University on the Gold Coast, before completing her postgraduate legal studies at the Australian National University and being admitted as an Australian lawyer in the ACT Supreme Court in 2014.

Jorja sees herself as a firecracker, a chaotic queen and a bogan with a penchant for nice things. She's a neurospicy ball of energy juggling several chronic health conditions (psoriasis, endometriosis, adenomyosis, secondary infertility), and is determined to show her little one that there are many ways around the roadblocks life throws at you. In her spare time, she's the ACT regional leader for The Nappy Collective, a foodie, a lover of drag shows and a cheerleader for other women in business.

You can connect with Jorja via social media: @theboujeebushpig

Learning to Fly

Kyah Seary

Finding my wings.

In life and in business, one of the biggest mistakes you can make is never having the courage to take flight. Fear is what holds most people back, but as a mother of three, CEO and founder of two of the largest gut health companies across the world, I can tell you that believing your self-doubt, listening to the negative voice in your ear or not jumping off the deep end when opportunity arises, is not how you become your highest self. In fact, it will leave you with regrets and a lifetime of wondering what could have been.

Myself personally? I don't let anything stand in my way. I don't want to wonder what I could have been, or what my life could have looked like if only I broke the cycle of 'the norm' and decided to live it. I once heard my father describing me to my husband after I told him what I'd been up to one night after dinner. After all, by this stage I had already moved across the world by myself at nineteen, leaving my family and friends behind in Seattle in search of adventure, sunshine and my destiny. I never felt I fit in there, always as if I'd already been put in a box of who I was supposed to become. My parents were successful academics. They were doctors and we lived in a nice house, in a nice neighbourhood. Of course, I went to a good school. But something inside me was screaming.

I wanted to wear my hippie skirt on a beach, in a foreign country where no-one knew my name. Where I never had to brush my hair or wear shoes if I didn't want to. I wanted to watch the sunset on the beach, do what made me happy, discover who I really was, and find my purpose. I decided to go to university in Australia, studying event and hotel management and fell in love with business and economics. The problem was, I didn't fit in the corporate box either. I hated wearing that hotel grey and gold pant suit more than anything and, once again, after starting work in hotels, I felt like a caged animal.

My best friend at the time, who was studying psychology, diagnosed my issue. She said I had a fear of being trapped and feeling boxed in, losing control and not having a choice.

Sounded about right to me. So what could I do? I had to work, I had to support myself.

FLAPPING MY WINGS LIKE HELL

Funnily enough, my dad always thought I would be an entrepreneur. I guess the theme seemed to be that I liked to beat to the rhythm of my own drum. But I never saw how this could relate to my career. Until I found my calling in colonics, which was my silver lining for all my gut issues as a teenager. Suddenly I knew exactly what I needed to do.

I learned the ropes, did my time learning my trade and instantly fell in love with clinic life. My wheels were already ticking, I could see room for improvement, and I knew one day, when the time was right, I would open my own space. And I would do it better.

That's exactly what I did. In 2018, five weeks before I gave birth to my son, I opened my first business. It was the best thing I ever did. Not only has it rewarded me financially, but more importantly, it allowed me to work from home to begin with, spend time with my kids, channel my passion, share my story with the world, grow and develop my skills in business, unleash my creativity and create an incredible community of like-minded people to share my life with. As a mother, starting my own business was the best thing for both my mental health and maintaining my identity, creating my own village for my children to grow up in.

I cannot tell you how incredible it has been to watch both my business and my children grow up, side by side. I went into labour with my second child on opening day at our first commercial space, my team holding down the fort as I birthed her naturally at home. A regular client took the phones and did reception until I was back on my feet a few months later. By the time I had my third, I had hired a manager to run the clinic while I began to take the reins of the e-commerce business I started in 2019 from home.

SOARING ABOVE THE CLOUDS

Scaling my business and my family (if you don't already know this … having two kids feels like having two kids. Having three kids feels like fifteen).

By the time I had my third baby, two years later, I had hired a manager to run the clinic full-time. With my new-found time and restless mind, I decided to use this maternity leave to pour some energy into our e-commerce business which was getting neglected.

The key with the online business was that it made at-home gut health solutions available to people all over the world, so we were no longer just bound to our one clinic space. This was essential for my business to scale and grow outside our walls, keeping us diversified and recession-proof, as the at-home options were more cost-effective and accessible for the everyday person.

Considering the entire world shut down for two years in 2020 … the timing could not have been better to focus on at-home solutions.

I took a course, made a few essential tweaks, learned how to write ads, got clarity and built a new website in a week. Then, I relaunched my brand, all while breastfeeding, waking with the baby a few times a night, day-care drop-off, bum-wiping and negotiating on the daily with my herd of children.

Overnight, my e-commerce business exploded. We quickly vaulted out of small business-hood and onto a whole new level. I was able to purchase our own office space and a second location for the colon hydro-therapy clinic. Long-term, it will create generational wealth for my family and leave a legacy for my children.

I flapped so hard, I flew … and you can too.

FLYING LESSONS – FROM ONE FREE SPIRIT TO ANOTHER

How I built two successful businesses and my best advice for any solo pilot looking to take flight in her own entrepreneurial career.

1. Build a brand, not a product or service.

One of the reasons my businesses have been so successful is because of the brands I created. It's what keeps you future-proof and always gives you a leg-up on your competition. It also sets the course for your business, as everything you do must come back to the vision, mission and values of the brand.

So, how do you build a brand? Start with the foundations. How do you want your products to make your customers feel? How does your brand talk to its customers? If there are two identical products, people will make their buying decisions based on which brand they align with most. So, you better make it a good one!

This has been absolutely instrumental in my e-commerce success, as everyone knows the online world is littered with look-alikes and cheap knock-offs. But what people remember about my brand is the packaging (this MATTERS!) and what your brand stands for. For us, it's all about taking something taboo, and previously shameful, and making it fun, supportive and empowering.

Our brand uses bright, uplifting and fun patterns that speak to the customers in a really inviting way, and any interaction they have with our customer service reflects this. People trust the brand more than the products themselves. It will create loyalty, a following, hype and a sense of belonging for your customers.

Think about your favourite brands ... what do you love about them? Why do you buy what you buy? Why do you go where you go? What feeling does that purchase bring you? New sportswear, a car, jewellery, your hair salon, your underwear? A candle ... is it luxury? Convenience? Indulgence? A sense of belonging? Environmental impact? Femininity? Each purchase you make is a choice and an energy exchange. Figure out why you want your customers to buy from you!

2. Create community.

More than ever in today's world, people are feeling isolated. Humans are designed for connection. We crave interaction, and you can cultivate this in your business. Whether it's a brick-and-mortar, client-based or e-commerce, you can create an online community that will grow your business, increase your client base and turn customers into lifelong fans. In my business, a huge issue for our customers was that they felt alone with their gut issues. They can be very embarrassing and they didn't have anyone to talk about them with ... until they found us!

So, we created an online Facebook group for our customers who had purchased our products; a safe space for people to ask questions, give encouragement and seek guidance from other people in the same position. We offer giveaways and interact with them personally, and it has been a beautiful way to further support and get feedback from our customers!

Social media is another great place to do this. Social media doesn't have to be a place to just share your pretty professional stock photos, it can be a place to engage with your customers, ask them questions, make them laugh, teach them things and show them what your brand is really about!

The more you engage your community, and learn about your customers, the more you will be able to make smart and informed decisions. We also launched an affiliate program to reward people for sharing our products and growing our community.

3. Be authentic.

Authenticity is so important in my opinion, because your customers are smart. They can feel the alignment with you and your brand, and how passionate you are in actually wanting to help them.

My own personal health battle led me to the business I created, and I share this with our customers because I feel it's important they know how genuine and passionate we are about what we offer.

One of the most rewarding feelings in the entire world is having a customer tell you how much your products or services have changed their life. It's why we do what we do. So be authentic, create something real and don't just do things for appearance.

4. You can do it all. Motherhood only makes you stronger.

I think many women feel intimidated by the idea of starting a business while they have children at home. Or even just the idea of entering what has so classically been a male-dominated sector. Or maybe you haven't had kids yet, but you're career-focused and not sure if you can do both, that it might hurt your success.

On the other hand, as a mother, you might think it will take away from your kids, your time, the house duties, and wonder how you will be able to manage both.

Hear this: *You can.*

The most challenging, life-altering and soul-defining experience of your life is giving birth. Bar none. Harness that. If you can give birth, raise kids and do all the things that you do, you can absolutely run a business. Your kids have prepared you for this – enabling you to make quick decisions, work on less sleep, work a budget and get creative in your negotiating skills.

It will be a juggle, but starting a business is like a newborn. The longer you nurture it, the more independent it becomes as it grows. You get what you put in and it's an incredible chance to create some freedom for your family, both financially and to be around for your kids.

I used to have one baby on the boob, a phone on my ear taking the bookings, stirring dinner, standing on one leg, bouncing up and down. I would do the accounting after the babies went down every night, had a babysitter come to the house for the first few years, so I could breastfeed in-between clients and usually started my day with emails from my phone at 4am while the baby fed. It was tough, but it was possible.

Being a mother can also make you highly relatable to your customers. In my businesses, I never hid my kids. They would sit on reception with me, come to meetings, help me pack orders, and I even made them a desk in my office. We welcome kids in our clinic and our business because we know how hard it is and that it takes a village. Motherhood is a club, and if your brand aligns with your customers' family values, it could be a big trust-builder for your audience! I will go out of my way to support another mum!

5. Build your freedom.

After building my business to a certain point, I was able to take a step back before I had my third baby. I actually stopped seeing clients myself, which was huge, and the business continued to grow. I had cultivated an amazing team and earned myself the freedom and time to now spend every day at home with the kids and work online from there.

The five years I initially invested in building my business to run on its own will now come back to serve me forever. It also gave me the freedom to expand my online business which funded the purchase of our very own clinic space this year. A forever home for our community and my first office to come play in, now that my kids are growing up and starting school.

YOUR BIGGEST ASSET

Wherever you are in your business journey, let me leave you with this. The greatest asset you will ever have, no matter your business size, is your own health. Never work so hard, run yourself down so much, that you put this in jeopardy.

From someone who struggled with chronic illness young in life, I know what it's like to not be able to accomplish the things you want to do because you are trapped in your body. As a business owner and a mother, you need your energy, a clear mind and a healthy body. For most, health only becomes of value once we throw it away. Treat yourselves with care and respect, that way you can go the distance with your business, keep up with your kids and enjoy all the blessings both will bring.

Move, eat well and poop every day, girlfriend. You've got this.

The world is waiting for you.

Xo

Kyah

Kyah Seary

Passionate colon hydrotherapist and a leader in wellness, Kyah Seary is a mother of three and the owner, CEO and founder of both Happy Bum Co and Bayside Colonics. Two of the largest detox and gut health businesses of their kind. She is leading a movement of change in gut health awareness and promotes the benefits of colon cleansing and using colonics and enemas as a part of a healthy lifestyle sharing her own authentic journey back to health using these lifesaving modalities.

After suffering extreme childhood constipation and feeling desperate for relief, Kyah fell in love with the benefits of detoxification. The pain she suffered kickstarted her passion for natural health, via enemas and colon cleansing.

Regular enemas became an important part of Kyah's tool kit in her gut healing journey as she suffered with colonic inertia. Providing immediate, natural and portable relief anytime, anywhere, Kyah couldn't believe no-one recommended this sooner.

After finishing her degree in business and studying colonics, she opened her own colon hydrotherapy clinic called Bayside Colonic in

Brisbane in 2018. Kyah could see there was a huge demand for this type of treatment and wanted to share her knowledge with the world.

By simply showing up every day on her social media and sharing her passion, uncovering the taboos of gut health, her story went viral and along with it her business.

After opening her clinic, Kyah saw a huge need for at-home enema kits to offer her clients. With nothing suitable on the market already, she was determined to change this and decided to create her own line of at-home detoxification and enema products to offer people worldwide, calling it the Happy Bum Co.

To combat the negative stigma and confusion surrounding enemas, the Happy Bum Co products are designed to provide their users with all the support, guidance and all the tools they need for success. Using only the best quality ingredients and equipment, Kyah's mission is to shift the mentality around enemas, making them an obvious natural choice to so many of today's health issues. In the process she has created an amazing community of like-minded people looking to better their health all over the world.

Today, the Happy Bum Co is a leader in the wellness industry, winning multiple awards including Best Wellness Product of the Year and now has warehouses in the US, UK and Australia. Her clinic Bayside Colonics has two locations and fifteen therapists providing treatment seven days a week.

In addition to running both of her businesses, Kyah is also a busy mother of three, wife and yogi. You'll find her at the beach with her fam when she's not at work! Kyah is also passionate about supporting women through their motherhood journey using her products and she found detoxification and gut health key in her own fertility. After three natural births, two waterbirths at home, she is a wealth of knowledge in this space and knows just how important self-care is as Mum!

How To Network, Collaborate And Build A Relationship-Based Business

As an Authentic Introvert

Lauren Micale

SO ... I'M AN INTROVERT ...

People assume I:

- Am shy.
- Am awkward.
- Can't hold an interesting conversation.
- Have RBF (resting b***h face – it's a thing!).

Don't get me wrong – some of those DO apply! I process the world in my head before speaking, I'm uncomfortable at large social events and meeting new people and would prefer to find a quiet corner and chat with one or two people.

The key for me to get through it, is to:

- Not overthink it.
- Be brave – just do it.
- Recover from the social hangover later (also a real thing!).

If you are part of my trusted inner circle, you will often hear me say, *I hate peopling.* That doesn't mean I hate people. I love a good chat and getting to know people – I just find it incredibly difficult when it feels forced and not about anything but the weather. Get me talking about a subject I'm passionate about and you'll be hard-pressed to shut me up!

My RBF makes me laugh (ironically!). It's just my face – minus my emotions – I'm processing everything internally before the expression of my thoughts makes its way externally to my face!

Let me tell you the story about how a dedicated, hardcore introvert mastered the art of networking, without being fake.

HOW IT STARTED

In 2014, I started my business with only one client. Networking was a scary word back then. Every time I considered it as a way to meet like-minded people, or prospective clients, I'd go into a spiral of overthinking and push it back to the bottom of the 'to-do' list.

Ten years later, I have over a hundred clients, a high-performing team and a business mostly based on building relationships and receiving referrals.

I still hate talking to strangers and going to social events … but I don't overthink it, I show up and do it and worry about recovering later.

I always loved working in accounts, office management and executive assistant (EA) roles. Behind the scenes, no small talk to make sales, none of the difficult management conversations, but still immersed in the business operations. I didn't want to have to fake a relationship to do business.

Being behind the scenes meant I connected with other EAs, accounts and office managers over emails and phone calls. We were just doing the work on behalf of someone else, so it was easy. There was an automatic connection already – an unspoken 'code' – that we would work together to get the job done. There was no pressure to build a relationship – those grew authentically and organically, all without leaving the comfort of my office.

It wasn't until many moons later (random aside – I'm what's known as a 'selenophile' – I love the moon – now there's a subject you can't shut me up about) that I realised those skills I was using daily were precisely the skills I needed to build my business. I'd been overthinking the whole process.

Building relationships can be as simple as having a conversation with one or two people, with the view of working on a common goal (even in a room full of people). If I thought about it as simply as that, it felt easy again.

BUSINESS – CONNECTING AND BUILDING RELATIONSHIPS

I own a virtual bookkeeping and admin practice. I needed to find clients and meet other people who could give me tips, guidance and connection, and help me with the skills I lacked.

But how could I find all this when I couldn't bear the thought of:

- Talking to strangers.
- Walking into a crowded room of strangers.
- Public speaking in front of a crowd (even for a thirty-second elevator pitch).

I joined a networking group.

(Little did I know then, I would meet many of my business besties through that networking group and its events, and eventually run a collaborative

co-operative venture with four of them.)

NETWORKING
Start small, but start

So, I joined the local networking group. I picked my favourite outfit (and changed my mind multiple times), including my big-girl pants, and worked on my elevator pitch. I had it down pat, I knew what I wanted to say.

With knocking knees, sweaty palms and a nervous smile, I packed my newly designed business cards, left the comfort of my office, walked in, ordered a cup of coffee and said 'hi' to the first friendly face I saw …

I just did it and refused to let myself give up and walk out.

I stood in front of what felt like a million people and introduced myself and my business …

I'm not going to lie; it was terrifying. I wanted to vomit, hide in the toilet and never come out again … I'm not sure how I didn't do that, but I do know my elevator pitch was delivered with quivering knees and voice (still is, to this day).

I realised that if I wanted to make my business successful, I needed to actively be brave, step into the 'arena' and talk to people. Tell them why I do what I do and explain how I can help them with my services and expertise.

FOCUS ON LISTENING

I ended up going to this networking event monthly. Instead of making sure I met everyone in the room and handing out business cards, I would find just one friendly face, say 'hi', ask about them and what they did. I realised it felt easier to ask about others instead of finding the words to tell someone upfront about what I did.

Next meeting, I would go and say 'hi' to everyone I'd met previously and extend the conversation in a casual way. Because I already knew them and what they did, I could be curious – ask more questions, get to know them better and form a connection. Then find someone new to say 'hi' to …

REPEATING THE PROCESS, BUILDING MY NETWORK, ONE PERSON AT A TIME

One of the key strategies that helped me be braver going to events was focusing on quality over quantity. I hated the awkward chitchat and card-swapping – it felt forced and 'salesy'. Instead of trying to meet as many people as possible, I consciously invested my time and energy with a few individuals, and genuinely found out about them and their business.

As I became more comfortable, I went to different networking events. It got a little easier every time. It would still all begin with wanting to vomit, and then I'd step out of my comfort zone – finding one person to talk to and asking about them and their business. I gained confidence through practice, and realised I could be an introvert and still share my services and build my business.

WHAT CAME LATER
Embrace your authenticity

As I got to know people and became more involved in the local business community, I discovered the power and joy of volunteering and giving back.

- I joined a committee to help organise a business expo.
- I became a host for that same networking event I was once so scared to go to.
- I collaborated on projects with other small businesses that shared

similar values.

These activities enriched my network and also allowed me to contribute to causes I believed in.

One of my biggest achievements to challenge my introversion in the early stages was becoming the co-host of that local networking group and volunteering on their management committee.

I created a welcoming environment, including for introverts like me, where everyone felt included and valued. I helped organise the monthly coffee events and spoke to local business owners to encourage attendance. I'd meet everyone who came to the events, and introduce the newbies to other long-time members, so they didn't have to stand alone or find the courage to walk up. Seeing how much I could help people who felt like I did built my confidence, so I could keep being brave each month.

I still have to stand up with shoulders back, take a deep breath, smile and just do it, but this gave me the opportunity to showcase my leadership skills and show my commitment to supporting the local business community. Knowing it's about helping others (and not so much about me), makes it easier to step up.

THE BEST THING ...

Through volunteering on these committees, I found myself continually growing more confident in navigating social situations and making meaningful connections. I also met people who inspired me to share my values and vision for success. I didn't expect this.

COLLABORATING

Focus on quality connections

Collaborating with others I've met during my journey has helped me exponentially grow my business. I no longer have to do everything. I work with others to achieve great results for my business. I always say 'focus on your best, outsource the rest' and this is what I do. Finding the right people is crucial. I wanted to work with people who have similar values to me. For example, I struggle to write content such as blogs (even this chapter!) but with the right collaboration I can make it happen. I focus on doing what I like best – numbers, numbers and more numbers – and work with others to make the rest of my business as successful as it can be. With people helping me in various parts of my business, I can do the things:

- I'm qualified for and have years of experience in.
- I enjoy doing.
- That help me to help others.

Whilst this has nothing to do with being an introvert, building collaborations is essential to a successful business, and unless I stepped up and started networking, I would never have found these other amazing businesses.

Some of the wonderful humans I met at networking events and on volunteer committees have blossomed into lifelong friendships and even business partnerships. One of these collaborative ventures I'm thrilled to be a part of is Sage Room Co-op. Alongside four other small businesses, we created the cooperative in 2022 to focus on sustainable small business growth and development.

Working together and thinking outside the box, we aim to show others that they can grow their businesses whilst maintaining their independence. We place great importance on wellbeing, happiness and a balanced life.

Through our services, products and spaces, we strive to support others – challenging traditional ways of working and encouraging other businesses to align with their values.

At Sage Room Co-op, we emphasise a creative and positive mindset, respecting each other's strengths and differences. We encourage people to look for and build quality relationships that collectively align for them. Together, we learn, grow and share our knowledge and experience to help others achieve their business goals and live their best life!

By working together, our network pools resources, knowledge and expertise to achieve goals more effectively. Collaboration fosters innovation and creativity, as our often very different perspectives combine to generate fresh ideas and solutions. We learn from each other's experiences and build stronger networks and relationships, giving access to a wider range of opportunities and support.

My journey has been considerably enhanced through collaboration, by leveraging all our collective strengths to overcome challenges, achieve common goals and create a positive impact on the world. Collaboration is a highly recommended tool for sustainable growth, and lots of fun along the way!

FAST-FORWARD A DECADE
Celebrate your successes
I'm proud to say my relationship-based approach to business has paid off in spades. What started with just one client back in 2014 has blossomed into a thriving business with over a hundred clients and a team of dedicated workers.

Here's the thing. I still struggle with networking, social events and talking to strangers. It's not easy, and there are days when I'd much rather hide in the comfort of my own home than put myself out there. But I've learned that success often lies just outside of your comfort zone.

So, I put on my 'big girl pants' and show up. I may feel anxious, awkward or downright terrified, but I do it anyway. Because I know the relationships and connections I build, and make, are worth all of it. In our co-op, not feeling up to 'peopling' is normal and supported. We prop each other up – sometimes attending events together or offering words of encouragement and always stretching.

If you're an introvert like me and nodding your head in agreement at these stories, here are a few tips to help you navigate the world of networking and build meaningful relationships in your business:

TIPS FOR INTROVERTED ENTREPRENEURS

- **Start small, but start:** Building relationships takes time. Don't expect instant results. Start small by attending local networking events or reaching out to individuals online. Seek out networking groups or communities where you feel comfortable and supported. Surround yourself with like-minded individuals who share your values and interests and watch your network grow organically.

- **Embrace your authenticity:** Don't try to be someone you're not. Instead, embrace your introverted nature and lean into your strengths. Authenticity is magnetic, and people will be drawn to you when you show up as your genuine self.

- **Focus on quality connections:** Instead of trying to meet as many people as possible, prioritise building genuine, meaningful relationships with a few individuals. In my experience relationships occur when you don't sell, you are authentic and are curious.

- **Focus on listening:** Instead of worrying about what you're going to say next, focus on truly listening to the people you're connecting with. Ask questions, show genuine interest and let the conversation flow naturally.

- **Celebrate your successes:** Acknowledge and celebrate your achievements, no matter how small they may seem. Each interaction and milestone is a testament to your resilience and growth as an introverted entrepreneur.

Looking back over the last decade, I can't help but feel grateful for the challenges I've faced as an introvert in the world of networking. While it hasn't always been easy, overcoming my fears and putting myself out there has been incredibly rewarding. I've learned that being an introvert doesn't have to hold you back from building a successful relationship-based business – it can be your greatest strength.

The most rewarding aspect of my journey has been the friendships I've formed along the way. Through shared experiences and mutual support, I've met some of my closest confidants and business allies. These relationships have enriched my personal life and opened doors to exciting new opportunities for my business.

So, to all my fellow introverts out there who may be struggling with networking; take a deep breath, put on those big girl pants of courageousness, and remember you have something valuable to offer the world. Embrace your introverted nature, lean into your strengths and don't be afraid to put yourself out there. You never know what amazing connections and opportunities are waiting for you on the other side of that initial discomfort.

Lauren Micale

L auren Micale is the founder and director of Bayside Admin & Bookkeeping.

She has been a virtual and executive assistant for over twenty years and has held numerous office, bookkeeping and account management roles. Her ability to turn chaos into clarity, with a smile that would calm an angry storm, is what keeps her client list growing! 'Once you have a Lauren, you can't imagine life without her,' is how one client described the experience of working with her.

Lauren has a bachelor of business management, certificate IV in accounting, and is a registered BAS agent and certified Xero advisor.

She is currently treasurer for Redlands Disability Network (RDN) has almost a decade of NDIS and disability sector accounts and administration experience, is a co-director of MGLA Consulting and a founding co-director with Sage Room Co-op Ltd.

You will find her (and her RBF) at lots of fun networking events throughout the year, talking about numbers, organising and maybe some fascinating facts about the moon! Check out her social pages to see just how many events she goes to and maybe she can be that friendly face for you one day when you walk in the door.

My Passion to Purpose

Lisa Schmelzkopf

Why as a mum and successful businesswoman do we lose who we are over time?

Are we inherently born with our passions, or do we unearth them through life's various milestones?

At the age of twelve I knew … I found myself drawn to concocting skin care remedies, experimenting with deep cleansing, exfoliation using sugar, moisturisers and blending different fruits with honey for diverse masks. This early inclination led me to aspire to help others with their skin concerns.

At the age of eighteen, I completed my diploma and secured my first position as a skin therapist, even prior to completing my final skin exam.

By the age of twenty-one, I opened my first day spa at Glenelg in Adelaide. Borrowing money from my Nanna for my skin care investment, whilst convincing my mother that I was never going to get married and to entrust me with my wedding funds *now*, so I could build my business. Lucky for me, she went along with it.

And so, my life in business began.

Hello to Abache Beauty in Glenelg, Adelaide.

PURPOSE & PASSION

I was lucky enough to have an exceptional mentor and colleague. Peter Francis, whose guidance was invaluable. He imparted the wisdom of business promotions, dream realisation and strategic planning.

I learnt how to cultivate a successful client base through hosting soirees/VIP nights every quarter, benefiting both the charities I supported and my day spa. These events would raise money for the chosen charity and add ten to twelve new facial clients to my day spa.

I established my reputation and brand through speaking at women's events and charities by advocating self-care and skin care expertise. It was a common occurrence for women reaching their forties or fifties to want to reinvent themselves, making it a priority in their life. They wanted to reverse those years of lying in the sun, to plump those fines lines or give themselves a much-needed hydration boost.

With a relentless schedule, my days commenced at 6am in the gym, extending to late hours concluding past 11pm some nights, immersed in planning, promotional endeavours and goal-setting. I was in my element; I loved it. My business was a success.

Amidst the hustle, there lingered little time for relationships, yet I would try every now and then, with a new love, but it would never work. It would always end in the same way; *You never have time for me,* he would say, or, *What time are you coming home? You're always at work.* Complaining, Complaining.

I will never get married and I will never have kids, I thought!

As my business grew, so did my passion. At age twenty-nine, I didn't want to just look after anti-aging clients. I was seeing more and more clients with skin conditions like dermatitis, eczema, acne, scarring and rosacea.

But it seemed to me that all the commercial skin care brands out there never really hit the mark. I trialled many different ranges in Australia, each promising a solution but exacerbating another like redness, flakiness or sensitivity.

Seeking a transformative skin care range, I journeyed to Bologna, Italy. I needed a skin care line that would create change quickly for my clients … and I wanted results.

I had also suffered from adult acne myself for the previous four years, so I needed something that would reduce the inflammation and stop the breakouts, but something that wasn't going to burn and strip the skin.

I found my answer in Centella and Hydraflore; a certified organic skin care line made in France – with no nasties.

Astonishingly, within three nights I had a remarkable improvement; reduced redness and inflammation. My skin was calmer and brighter, and wasn't sore to touch.

I imported the line back to Australia and my clients loved it. They would walk out of the treatment room into my waiting room, where there was a glass ceiling, as well as a floor-to-ceiling mirror … and their jaw would drop! They were so impressed, they could see the change in their skin after just one treatment.

So out with the commercial brands and on with our new journey: Centella.

Funnily enough, that's when I also met the love of my life, Dominic. He was everything I could have dreamed of.

He gave me space to achieve my work goals; we would have business discussions most nights over wine. We would bounce ideas off each other and he supported my dream without complaining. But guess what happened – I wanted to get married. I wanted to have a child. So after about eight weeks of dating, I gave him the two-year plan; a step-by-step conversation of what I wanted and *if he didn't agree,* then we needed to go our separate ways. Lucky for me, he went along with the plan.

And months later our daughter, Ruby Scarlett, was born.

At the same time as motherhood, I wanted my skin clinic too … I can do both, right? I believed I could manage them both seamlessly. I'm invincible! Twelve years' experience as a successful day spa owner, I could do it with my eyes closed. And looking after a newborn couldn't be that hard, could it?

My daughter was born, along with my second business, Centella Skin and Wellness clinic, in Glenelg, Adelaide. This is when my world started to change, the reality of balancing motherhood, entrepreneurship and personal aspirations proved daunting.

Sleep deprivation, absence of maternity leave and relinquishing breastfeeding after four weeks painted a chaotic picture; a far cry from my youthful resilience. Struggling to juggle a myriad of responsibilities, I found myself overwhelmed and fragmented, gradually losing pieces of myself amidst the demands of motherhood and business ownership. As a mother navigating the world and building a business, the constant juggling act left me questioning why women lose themselves in the pursuit of balance.

At six weeks old, my daughter entered child care, a transition I wasn't prepared for. My father, a 'baby whisperer', cared for Ruby Scarlett every Saturday, as both Dominic and I both had businesses that were open on Saturdays. I didn't get to go to the gym. I didn't get to work *on* my business, only *in* it. The strain left me drained emotionally, grappling with the toughest period of my life.

The conflict between nurturing and wanting to spend all my time with Ruby Scarlett, and fulfilling professional responsibilities, weighed heavily on me. The guilt was palpable, business demands clashed with maternal instincts.

By the age of sixteen months, Ruby Scarlett had enough of going to Grandpa's on Saturdays after a full week of child care. She was screaming because all she wanted was her mumma. It was heart-wrenching.

My anxiety set in. In a whirlwind, my head was spinning, and I was now reacting, instead of planning and smashing goals. You can't eat, you're lost … you haven't come up for air. You discover you don't know how to do anything anymore. In the blink of eye, time has passed and you haven't even realised.

Selling my business became imperative; I had to prioritise Saturdays with my baby. We needed something different! Work hours had to be Monday to Friday.

And so, my third business, SC Organics was born. An Adelaide-based wholesale skin care company specialising in Centella and Hydraflore. The certified organic skin care line from France that provides results-driven facial and body treatments, and prescribed home care. I now get to share my twenty-five years of proven knowledge, fostering business growth, helping our Centella stockists to increase their business.

We welcomed the arrival of our second daughter, cheeky Coco Emily. My snuggly little affectionate go-getter, who looks exactly like me. The juggling act resumed, back to broken sleep and less resistance on my behalf.

With two young girls, I felt torn every time I left home to go to the airport, travelling to Sydney to support our salons. Tears shed on the plane, missing both my girls terribly, I was guttered all over again. Why do we do this to ourselves?

Why did motherhood and entrepreneurship necessitate such sacrifices?

It's taken me twelve years to realise how to navigate smarter; striving to balance family, sanity and professional aspirations. How to find that balanced, happy-go-lucky me again.

Why as a mum and successful businesswoman do we lose who we are over time? Why do we become lost? The clarity of the path fades, we're second-guessing ourselves, reacting to circumstances. I felt like a tiger trapped in a cage. I felt constant guilt when it came to my daughters, feeling split in half emotionally and mentally, wanting to work on my business but still be the best mum I could be.

I would continuously ask myself:

What is the ideal mum I want to be?

What is the ideal person I want to become?

I'm dedicating this upcoming section to all the 'mumpreneurs' out there who are seeking balance with their family and to help you find yourself again.

MY TOP TIPS THAT HAVE WORKED FOR ME OVER TIME

1. Scheduling time.

Begin your day early to accommodate personal and professional commitments. I like to be free for two school drop-offs and pickups. Most days starting at 5:15am, I'm in the office until 6:30am, then I get ready with the kids and do school drop-off, gym or self-care activities and my workday officially starts at 11am. This allows me to accomplish tasks efficiently before the day begins. And even though I'm only working for an hour or so while everyone is still sleeping, for me, it is the equivalent of three hours of work.

This allows me to priority my tasks and I feel I'm on top of things.

2. Work in blocks of time.

Organise your schedule in blocks, ensuring dedicated time for family engagement, alongside work commitments.

I block out my diary for everything, reminding myself not to take that 3pm meeting because I have school pickup that day and to be present in my kid's activities. Being self-employed, you don't have to work 9am-5pm or for twelve hours a day. You can schedule the school assembly in your diary. You can attend every school event to make the kids feel important and to fill up your own emotional cup. I go to all the sports days and all the important events. I'm even on the parents and friends board because it makes me feel closer to my kids at school. It sounds funny but I treat all the school events just as importantly as my salon meetings.

3. Travelling for work.

Incorporate family into business travel whenever possible. Most of my larger trips of four days or more, I always include my family. I get to do what I love and my family gets to see another part of the world. I'm lucky that Dominic supports me on that, otherwise I don't think I would go.

4. To ease the guilt.

The answer for me is balance. Seek balance by alternating between work tasks and quality time with your children. What makes them feel special?

I recently took a Centella training workshop for another skin care company in Singapore and, of course, my family joined me. The deal was, every day that I worked in Singapore would be a day my girls could choose the activity we would do as a family. They have learned to give and take. Encourage mutual understanding and compromise within your family dynamics.

5. After-school care; use it, they love it!

Embrace after-school care services to facilitate uninterrupted work or personal time. I use that hour, 4:30-5:30pm and utilise this window for meetings or to prepare dinner, so when they come home at 6:15pm, I can prioritise my family interactions.

6. Making time for yourself.

I attend one or two retreats or business conferences annually. This gives me time out. I'm around like-minded people, I'm motivated and it clears my head. It allows me to download and to be inspired. I come home a new woman.

7. Massages.

Massages are key for me. Prioritise spiritual and physical wellbeing. Find a place that not only eases the tension from your muscles but also helps you spiritually. Clears the mind and helps to shift any negativity. My girls have grown up attending all those massage sessions and they love it because they get to lay in the waiting area and watch a movie on their iPad and be spoilt with a few lollies from the owner.

8. Transform yourself regularly.

Embrace change periodically. This is a big one for me. I tend to do this a couple times of year. Going from long hair to short hair. Invest in a new look, shopping sprees, even if you can't afford it, you deserve it. I find it puts a pep back in my step and the better you feel, the better you perform.

9. Spend the day in bed.

Schedule downtime to disconnect from responsibilities and indulge in personal rejuvenation. A day when you can turn the phone off, your kids might be at sport and you have organised someone else to do the sport runs that day, or you have chosen to have a mental health day. Don't tell anyone. Just do it and binge, watch something on Netflix. Just stop! And recharge.

10. Find what makes you happy.

What's good for your soul? Identify activities that bring you joy and fulfilment. For me, I enjoy a day of cooking. Pouring that glass of wine on a Sunday afternoon and cooking up storm. Cooking three dishes in one day. Not only do I enjoy that time in the kitchen, but I also have a beautiful family lunch and you get to have meals ready for the next few days.

11. Write it down.

When you feel lost in both success and emotional direction, document your aspirations and the pathway to them. Journalling is pivotal, offering new insights into your desired achievements.

I do this and use this as a map to get back on track. Have a secret journal that no-one knows about. And let yourself shine again.

12. Let's talk anxiety.

Let's delve into anxiety. Some label it as weakness; I perceive it as a bridge to your next life's phase. It manifests as an inability to cope: constricted chest, breathlessness and scattered thoughts – you just want to hide. Responsibilities tether you. Echoing my own experiences, commit to morning exercise, even a walk, for clarity. Tune into motivational podcasts for solidarity. Persevere – the struggle is worthwhile. You'll emerge stronger on the other side. Believe in yourself. Push through!

13. Facials.

Of course, visit your favourite Centella clinic where you get to immerse yourself in the beauty bed while they perform your certified organic facial treatment. Invest in self-care, you will feel revived and renewed, plus your skin will look amazing.

Remember to prioritise your own happiness and wellbeing, as a content and fulfilled parent translates to a happier family environment. Take time to reflect on your needs and aspirations, ensuring alignment between your personal and professional life for optimal fulfilment.

I trust this reflection has provided you with valuable insights, prompting a pause for introspection regarding your emotions. Consider how you envision your family dynamics and the ideal shape of your professional endeavours. Balancing these aspects is essential for maternal fulfilment, prioritising your own wellbeing benefits both you and your children, fostering a happier, radiant environment.

scorganics.com.au & scorganics.com.au/pages/our-stockists

Lisa Schmelzkopf

Lisa Schmelzkopf is a renowned figure in the beauty and wellness industry, celebrated for her outstanding achievements and unwavering commitment to excellence. With notable accolades such as being awarded Best Beauty Therapist in South Australia in 2005, Lisa's journey as a trailblazer has been marked by a passion for empowering women and fostering growth within the business community.

A mother of two and a finalist for the Mum Entrepreneur Award, Lisa's expertise is undeniable. She co-founded the first Women in Business Networking Association for the Southern Business Enterprise, showcasing her dedication to supporting and uplifting women in the professional sphere.

Lisa's entrepreneurial spirit shines through her successful ventures, including a thriving day spa in Glenelg and a renowned skin and wellness clinic. Her journey as the owner and director of SC Organics, based in Adelaide, South Australia, reflects over twenty-five years of invaluable experience and a commitment to redefining industry standards.

Lisa's expertise in assisting the development of day spas, skin clinics and salons across Australia is unmatched, with a proven track record of significantly increasing salon turnover within the first year. Internationally recognised as an industry luminary, Lisa's passion for skin care is evident in every meticulously crafted treatment tailored to deliver transformative experiences for all skin types and conditions.

As a true nurturer, Lisa ensures each client receives a personalised journey of luxury and rejuvenation, guiding them towards their skin care goals with precision and care. Her commitment extends to cultivating a dynamic team of exclusive stockists, equipped with the knowledge and skills to drive transformative change in every encounter.

Innovation, empathy and unwavering excellence define Lisa Schmelzkopf's legacy in the realm of skin care, leaving an indelible mark on the industry and the lives she touches. Her story of vision, drive and dedication serves as an inspiration to aspiring entrepreneurs and professionals alike, making her a sought-after speaker for public events focused on business, wellness and women's empowerment.

scorganics.com.au

I'm Not Tinkerbell so Don't Expect Fairy Dust

Melissa Stehr

If you were to ask my team for a regular phrase that comes out of my mouth, I would bank on at least one of them to say: *I don't do fluffy!* Whilst writing this I was reflecting on my journey and what has led me to be an entrepreneur and woman in business.

How did I get to a place in my life where I understood my purpose and passion?

My first inside exposure to entrepreneurship was when I was in single digits. Around the age of seven, my parents bought a rundown takeaway shop in a small town on the Wide Bay Coast of Queensland.

The idea of purchasing the shop was twofold for my parents; it had a dwelling behind the shop that was enough for us to live comfortably and make a home, and the shop provided employment for both my parents.

I don't know if they had a 'game plan' around turning it around and selling it, or if they just went with the flow. What I do know is, through this opportunity, and through my parents, I saw a great example of what living with purpose and passion looks like.

My dad would often talk to my siblings and me about 'purpose'. He would rouse us if we were 'slacking' in our work. He would always say,

PURPOSE & PASSION

Walk with purpose, or else it looks like you don't know where you are going. And if you don't know where you are going, no-one will ever want to follow you.

He would then further that by saying we needed to take purpose with us through life:

Work with purpose. Talk with purpose. Love with purpose. Act with purpose. I still today use this insight with myself, with my adult sons and across my teams at work.

My passion is an easy one. I love people. I love seeing people be happy. Truly, cheek to cheek – smile happy. I love people achieving more than they believed and living in their own 'genius' spot.

Being married and a mother at the age of eighteen certainly required me to grow up quickly. I met my husband in the last year of school. He is one of the most amazing people I've ever met, and I knew I had to have a life with him in it.

The power of people is one I believe that is underestimated in everyday life. The value we can add to other people's lives and the appreciation of others in our life is a reality in my everyday existence. I am super protective of my 'presence'.

Lessons I've learnt along the journey of marriage, motherhood and as a business owner are what make me who I am today and are what will continue to make me the woman I will always strive to be.

I choose to be proud of myself and my achievements thus far. Knowing where I have come from, I truly have a limitless belief of what I can achieve.

I choose to make me happy and reflect on my awesomeness. This is how I believe I can make a positive impact, which is why I have such a strong sense of purpose and passion around my presence. I am a gift, and therefore I should BE A GIFT to others.

Melissa Stehr

Melissa's childhood was predominantly spent in central Queensland, Australia. Moving to the Sunshine Coast with her family to finish year twelve, she met her now-husband at high school. Melissa married Nicholas in 1995. Fast-forward to 2007, three sons and now living in Melbourne, Victoria, Melissa and Nick purchased their first business, HLS Healthcare.

In 2024, HLS Healthcare has grown from a three-person business to thirty-eight people.

Melissa currently holds the position of CEO at HLS.

In 2015, Melissa drew on her passion from the exposure across the health care industry and disability sector and founded Access Advisor Australia. Their mission is to break down barriers that exist by increasing awareness for an improved, inclusive and accessible Australia. They connect the supplier with the consumer with transparent information about offerings – 'Know before you Go'.

Melissa enjoys her time providing private business coaching and supporting entrepreneurs who seek growth and success. Melissa is a member of the Forbes Club Australia and regularly voluntarily chairs at networking events in her local area.

Out of the Shadows and into the Spotlight

Melony Cherrett

Growing up in the nineties in Sydney, Australia, as one of the only mixed-race girls with freckles, almond-shaped eyes and muscular legs, from a young age, I felt the weight of society's narrow standards of beauty press upon me. I was often the target of hurtful words. The whispers and taunts made me want to shrink, to hide my Indonesian heritage and yearn for a different reflection in the mirror. The feeling of being an outsider, of not fitting in, haunted me. I was hesitant to embrace my uniqueness, feeling that, because of the way I looked, I had nothing valuable to offer.

However, when I discovered dance and singing at the age of twelve, I found a part of me I was willing to show to others. Dance became my safe space; a place where I felt comfortable being seen. Upon leaving high school, I attended a full-time performing arts school, and here, I was confronted with the competitive nature of dance. This industry is all about being seen, but my insecurities held me back from grasping opportunities. The competitive spirit of the dance world threatened to extinguish that spark. Comparison and self-doubt began to cloud my love.

Dance has always been my sanctuary; a space where I lose myself, free from the persistent chatter of the mind. Yet, my insecurities held me back from fully embracing my passion. However, that changed in a pivotal moment during a mock audition. Filled with nerves and self-doubt, I got dressed in a red leotard, put my hair in pigtail plaits, laced up my jazz shoes and prepared to head into an arena of competition and comparison. I stood in front of a panel amid rows of other dancers who all seemed confident, as if they already had the part. One of my mentors, who I admired and almost feared because of his presence, knowledge and talent, was sitting right in the centre.

I poured my heart into that audition, dancing like never before. I wasn't afraid to be seen. I wasn't afraid to be different. To my astonishment, I received that coveted callback. My mentor's words from that day still resonate deeply within me: *There were girls in the front, girls in the back, and then there was you. You were different. Your technique wasn't the strongest, but I couldn't take my eyes off you. Yes, to the callback!* His words were a revelation, teaching me that standing out isn't about vying for the front row but about embracing presence, bravery and seizing opportunities to shine in your unique way.

Fate intervened when my mentor, the very person who had inspired and guided me, became my choreographer for a dream role as a showgirl on cruise ships. I always had a desire to leave Australia and immerse myself in culture and experiences overseas and working on cruise ships would allow me to do this. His unwavering belief in me drove my confidence to audition for a role typically reserved for tall, statuesque dancers. After sending off my audition tape, I was thrilled to learn I had secured the job, marking the beginning of an extraordinary journey. Rehearsals in London were just the start, then I embarked on my first contract at sea and instantly fell in love with it. After three years, my first adventure came to an end, my heart was full, and I'd met the person I wanted to spend my life with. We decided to head back to land and moved to London with little savings and threw ourselves back into the world of auditioning hoping to score roles on London's West End. The multitude of auditions thrust me back into the world of self-doubt and comparison. One night after trekking through the snow on route to a friend's house, my now-husband and I sat on a supermarket bench eating marked-down food and I looked at him and said, *I can't do this anymore. I can't be turned down again and again. I want to go back to the ships.*

Just days before I was set to leave for the Caribbean, a last-minute change turned everything on its head. My partner and I had each secured contracts on different ships, a fact we'd reluctantly accepted due to our need for financial stability. He was bound for Brazil, and I was heading to the Caribbean. We had accepted the fact that our reunion would have to wait until the contracts ended in nine months.

Four days before my departure, however, an unexpected call from my agent brought news that shifted our plans entirely. *There's been a change*, he said. *You've been promoted to dance captain, and there's also been a reshuffling of contract placements. You're now scheduled for the same ship as your partner. And you'll be flying out to Brazil next week!*

During this time, I had the opportunity to be with my partner and sail to numerous destinations, immersing myself in diverse cultures and living alongside people from over forty different countries. It was a vibrant melting pot, where everyone was welcomed into each other's worlds. Bonds were forged, and we became like family, embracing and sharing our unique cultural backgrounds. For the first time, I felt a profound sense of belonging, finding my place in this global community.

We decided to head to Australia, but instead of feeling at home, there was a void and yearning for connection and purpose; I missed dancing.

PURPOSE & PASSION

Seeking a dance community that resonated with me, I found none. It was my husband's inspired suggestion that ignited a spark: *Why not create your own?* And so, fuelled by my passion and a vision to empower others through dance, I embarked on a new journey.

Embracing my own journey of rediscovering confidence and wanting to create a dance space where comparison and perfection didn't exist, I envisioned a class that would inspire others, regardless of their dance experience, age, shape or size. Drawing inspiration from my love for Broadway jazz and commercial styles, and my new-found passion for burlesque, I crafted an accessible blend of burlesque fusion classes. These classes celebrated the art of embracing every facet of oneself, focusing not on perfection, but on unleashing one's alter ego and embracing authenticity and having a whole lot of fun doing it!

Armed with nothing but passion and a vision, my business was born. Despite my lack of business experience, I was determined to create a space where individuals could connect, grow and celebrate their unique selves through the transformative power of dance.

In my quest to build a dance community, I embarked on a humble journey that began with just six women, gathered through friends, word of mouth and a less-than-perfect homemade flyer. Despite the perception many may have of me now as a dancer and the founder of a national brand, few know the hesitations and self-doubt that almost derailed my first class. Imposter syndrome consumed me, leading to an emotional breakdown filled with doubts: *No-one will like me. They'll hate my routines. I can't choreograph.* Yet, as any seasoned performer knows, *The show must go on!*

As those six brave women arrived for that first class, I greeted them with a smile, masking my internal insecurities. As we stood in a circle for our first pose, I felt a shift – a collective energy, a sanctuary to shed our nine-to-five personas, release body insecurities and rediscover the joy and laughter of childhood. Through burlesque fusion, we embarked on a journey of self-love and acceptance, a transformative experience I had only recently started to discover myself.

This journey, however, was not without its challenges. Shortly after launching my business, I found myself navigating the complexities of pregnancy and the birthing of two babies: my daughter and my business. Whilst I had a relatively smooth pregnancy, little did I know the challenges that lay ahead – a road marked by health struggles and postnatal anxiety.

My traumatic birth experience and my first daughter's health struggles weighed heavily on me, fuelling my anxiety and overshadowing my new-found motherhood. Despite the signs, I kept going. I wasn't sleeping, my daughter had some health issues and wasn't gaining weight. After many paediatric appointments and still not finding any answers, I began to spiral into the world of health anxiety. I wasn't sleeping and would stand over her bassinet night after night checking if she was breathing. I continued to neglect my wellbeing and pretended everything was okay, until a terrifying panic attack in public which forced me to confront my anxiety head-on.

Accepting my anxiety diagnosis was a challenging and ongoing process. I built a support network of health professionals, friends and family and started to rebuild myself. This personal journey deepened my understanding of the struggles that many women and mothers face – struggles that often go unnoticed and unspoken. Having a voice and a sense of relief in being able to talk about my mental health struggles allowed me to move into my second pregnancy with a plan. My second birth healed me. I found trust in my body and was able to birth my second daughter without the fear of having the same traumatic experience and aftermath that occurred with my first daughter. I now had two beautiful daughters and something inside me ignited. I wanted them both to grow up in a world where they didn't have to be faced with comparison, shame and uncertainty each day of their lives – like I experienced growing up.

Rediscovering dance, now as a mother of two, reconnected me with my purpose and passion, not only for dance, but also my business. I finally begun to understand that despite the uniqueness of each person's journey, there's a common desire to reconnect with oneself, to exist beyond the roles of mother or wife, and to simply be in the present moment, even if just during an hour-long dance class.

Inspired by these insights, I forged ahead, determined to provide an accessible space where others could find solace and empowerment through dance. Our burlesque fusion classes expanded to suburbs all around Adelaide, allowing time-poor women to attend a class close to home rather than having to travel into the city. Witnessing the courage of our community members as they stepped onto the stage for the first time, baring their vulnerabilities in corsets and suspenders, was a testament to the power of dance, as a tool for empowerment and self-discovery.

When someone steps onto the stage for their first show, the transformation is a mix of empowerment, adrenaline, acceptance and profound self-love. It's as if the spotlight not only shines on them, but also ignites a dormant light within, revealing their inner strength and beauty. Witnessing and being part of this transformative experience within our community is not just rewarding, it's a beautiful affirmation of our shared humanity and resilience.

Over the years, I've had the immense privilege of immersing myself in the personal narratives of many individuals and witnessing their profound transformations through my business. It became apparent, that while dance was a significant catalyst, the true power lay in the collective stories that bound them together. Recognising the importance of these experiences, I felt a compelling urge to share them, believing they could inspire others on their journeys of self-discovery.

For a long time, I urged my husband, a filmmaker, to document our vibrant community. It wasn't until he attended one of our dress rehearsals to capture some footage that he truly understood the impact of our business and how it was changing people's lives. Watching the passion and emotion on display, he turned to me and said, *Let's do it. I'll take time off work, and we'll go all-in.*

We reached out to our community, inviting them to share their stories of transformation. The response was overwhelming, with over four hundred members contributing their deeply personal tales. Reading each story, we were filled with laughter and tears, and were instilled with a sense of pride and admiration for their courage. Driven by our passion, we self-funded the documentary, naming it *Unleash*. Despite the uncertainties of its reception and path, we knew it deserved an audience.

After completing the film, we faced rejection from multiple distribution companies due to our lack of prior credits and notoriety. Undeterred, we forged our own path and managed to secure screenings in Australian cinemas. The film resonated deeply, playing to sold-out audiences and capturing the hearts of many. This success caught the attention of one of the very distribution companies who had initially turned us down. Impressed by our determination and the film's impact, they agreed to distribute *Unleash,* and connect us with international distributors, which led us to a path where our passion piece is now available on streaming platforms worldwide.

Bringing *Unleash* to life was fraught with challenges and moments of doubt. There were times when anxiety loomed large, and we questioned our capacity to manage such an ambitious project. Yet, our belief in the transformative power of sharing these stories drove us tirelessly forward. This unwavering commitment not only brought *Unleash* into existence but also helped it find its rightful place in the world, proving that even the most daunting obstacles can be overcome with perseverance and passion.

My businesses growth and development has been a testament to the transformative power of perseverance and unwavering belief in our vision. Despite the sacrifices, living off $30 a week and being brought food parcels, missing weekend getaways and catch-ups with friends, we channelled our passion and dedication into creating a community where individuals could discover and embrace their authentic selves.

I've learned to navigate the ebbs and flows of anxiety, finding strength in engaging with loved ones and focusing on tasks that align with my purpose. While the road has been fraught with challenges, it has also been incredibly rewarding. Our community has grown beyond our wildest dreams, with a national team of over fifty wonderfully aligned staff and contractors, and thousands of individuals stepping into their own spotlights across Australia each week.

Reflecting on this incredible journey, one truth shines brightly: the joy of witnessing others unlock their inner light and embrace their true potential surpasses any challenge or sacrifice endured along the way.

As I gaze into the mirror, my freckled face adorned with a few more wrinkles, standing at my unaltered height of 5'2" with muscular legs and a body that has birthed two children, I see a woman who has learned to embrace every part of herself. My hope is that each person reading this is inspired to pursue their own dreams, whatever they may be. Whether it's burlesque fusion, art, writing or any passion that stirs your soul, dare to step outside your comfort zone.

Don't stand in the shadows, for when you stand beneath your own spotlight, you illuminate the beautiful, unique and unapologetically authentic parts of yourself.

Melony Cherrett

Melony Cherrett resides in Adelaide, South Australia. She is the owner of Choo La La Burlesque Fusion, a wife, a mother of two beautiful girls and two Frenchie pugs.

Melony's journey to becoming a beacon of empowerment and creativity began with a passion for dance and performance. After a fulfilling career as a professional dancer and singer on cruise ships, Melony felt a calling to create something extraordinary – a community where individuals could express themselves freely and confidently. This vision gave birth to Choo La La, a burlesque-fusion dance community that has since grown exponentially, encompassing thousands of members across Australia.

Melony's philosophy at the heart of Choo La La is simple yet profound: every person possesses an innate ability to discover their inner confidence and shine brightly on stage. Despite facing challenges herself, particularly being deemed 'too short' at a height of only 5'2", Melony defied societal norms and carved out a successful career as a showgirl. Her personal experiences fuelled her determination to ensure that nobody should feel discouraged or limited by stereotypes.

As the founder and creative director of Choo La La, Melony has been instrumental in fostering a supportive and inclusive environment where members can explore their creativity, build self-confidence and embrace their unique identities. Her commitment to empowering others has extended beyond the dance studio, leading her to serve as the creative director for the feature documentary *Unleash.*

Released in 2021, *Unleash* chronicles the transformative journeys of twelve women from the Choo La La community. The documentary was met with overwhelming support, screening to sold-out audiences in cinemas across Australia. In 2024, *Unleash* made its television premiere on SBS Viceland and became accessible to a global audience through streaming platforms like Amazon Prime UK.

The profound impact of Melony's work with Choo La La is evident in the countless testimonials from women who credit the community in being a safe space that helps them overcome body image issues, combat isolation and navigate various life challenges. Through her passion, resilience and unwavering belief in the power of self-expression, self-acceptance and self-love, Melony continues to inspire and uplift individuals, proving that with determination and support, anyone can unleash their inner strength, confidence and come home to themselves via the stage.

sbs.com.au/ondemand/movie/unleash/2309626947991
choolala.com.au

Conversations With Myself

Morium Khan

To my grandfather,
Who, during his time in this world, saw beyond any 'isms
Who believed in me to soar my wings beyond any horizon.

The start of life marks something unchosen and untold.
It is through life itself, that we make choices and tell our stories.
Narate as you wish.

My life began in a place where life often ends, amongst one of the poorest countries in the world.

In the early nineties, after my family migrated to Australia, I faced every 'ism' imaginable. The odds were not in my favour.

My earliest memory is from year two, when I was the darkest kid in class. The other children's constant remarks about my 'poopy coloured curry' and 'mud-caked skin' culminated in a child placing a pin upside down on my chair, hidden by a ball of Blu-tack. Things could have been gruesome without one bully's stronger conscience than the others.

Deidre whispered, 'You don't belong here.'

As the daughter of Bengali immigrants, I worked hard. Early on, at home, we were forbidden from speaking in English – a well-concerted ode to sustaining a limb of the East's tradition while basking in the glory of the West. I didn't fully grasp the English language until my latter single digits. Until then, I was often a silent mime, following the gestures and cues of others just to keep up.

To compensate, I began memorising dictionary words and their definitions, until I realised I was getting good at only 'A' words in public conversations. Alas! I found myself achingly adrift in an amalgam of ambiguous As.

Deidre chuckled, 'They'll never understand you.'

Therefore, I worked hard – studying in three-hour blocks without breaks. This wasn't born from innate motivation, but from a family friend's claim that her daughter studied for three hours daily. My mother's horrified reaction led to a late-night scolding for being a 'lazy, useless daughter', and my early Saturday mornings never looked brighter after that.

Despite my best efforts, I failed Western Australia's GATE testing through a cruel twist of fate – I'd coloured an answer in the previous question's bubble, setting off a domino effect that derailed the entire exam. Facing my parents afterward, I had more explaining to do than a politician caught in a scandal.

My family also lived outside 'good school' zones, so my chance of accessing a quality education seemed grim. Each weekend, I pored over the newspaper's pages, marvelling at the achievements of those whose names were synonymous with excellence. I noticed that the state's highest achievers were often products of exclusive private schools, their success stories like bright dots scattered across the educational landscape. These institutions, with their well-resourced environments and exceptional teaching staff, seemed worlds apart from the public schools I knew. This saddened me, but it did not surprise me. The inequity was a constant reminder that where you lived and the school you attended could significantly influence your future.

I wanted to be a top student like them, but my relatively modest upbringing meant that my only ticket to high-quality education was through a scholarship. I dedicated school lunchtimes to learning better English and arranged after-school meetings with teachers for further practice.

At the scholarship testing for St Hilda's, I watched hundreds of girls compete for four places. The air was thick with nervous energy and competitive tension. The sound of pencils scratching on paper filled the room, punctuated by occasional sighs and the rustle of turning pages. As I jumped from question to question, I began to question myself more and more. There were so many answers I didn't know, not because I hadn't studied, but because I'd never been taught them.

Deidre's voice grew louder, 'You're not good enough, that's why.'

The writing task called for a narrative of transformation. I penned a tale of a child, much like myself, raised in a household where rote learning and perfect scores eclipsed the joy of play. This character, once resentful of the relentless pursuit of academic excellence, gradually discovered the quiet satisfaction of disciplined study. Resistance became resilience; expectations evolved into self-driven curiosity. Through this narrative, I pledged my own metamorphosis – if granted this scholarship, I'd cherish learning as a privilege, not a chore. It would be my catalyst for growth, honoured through unwavering dedication.

This audacious gambit unlocked the gates to St Hilda's.

Be truthful, passionate and daring – you won't regret it.

This same boldness led me to a defining moment of youthful audacity. Children were invited to perform at a mid-nineties cultural showcase, a time synonymous with Spice Girls, Tamagotchis, and dial-up internet. Amidst a sea of practiced talents, there I stood – five years old, brimming with nothing but raw optimism. Driven by an unnamed force (we'd later call it FOMO), I declared with unwavering conviction, *I'll play the piano.*

As the night grew older, it was my turn to dazzle. I pranced across the stage with the enthusiasm of a caffeinated squirrel, channelling the spirits of Mozart, Beethoven and Chopin – or so my vivid imagination believed. My fingers danced a chaotic ballet across the keys, composing a symphony only a child's heart could appreciate. Just as my 'masterpiece' reached its peak, my father's voice, seated at the back of the crowd, cut through the cacophony: *That's enough, Morium; you can sit down now!*

The silence that followed was deafening, a void filled only by the burning of my cheeks and the thunderous pounding of my heart. As I ran across the stage, seeking the comfort of solitude, I heard whispers, awkward claps and laughter that set my soul on fire.

It would be a very long time before I agreed to go on stage again.

Even then, this moment taught me the boundless power of a child's mind – where impossibility doesn't exist. In moments of doubt, I return to that fearless five-year-old, who reminds me that with imagination and an unwavering belief – anything is possible. For in the realm of dreams, we can all play beautiful music. Show up for yourself and believe you can – because you truly can.

Some of the most notable lessons I learned were from strangers.

At thirteen, waiting for my mother after a workshop on learning combinatorics and differential equations, I met a girl with a worn leather jacket and a powerful message. Her eyes held a wisdom beyond her years, and there was a quiet confidence in her demeanour that drew me in. She told me how, succumbing to family pressures, she had wasted five years studying engineering, only to realise her true passion was teaching. *Don't make my mistake*, she urged, her voice a mix of regret and determination. *Tread carefully, but tread your own path.*

Her simple yet profound message – to honour one's authentic self while respecting the delicate balance of ambition and wisdom – would become the cornerstone of both my personal philosophy and business ethos.

In 2011, as part of my law degree, I returned to Bangladesh to work with Dr Kamal Hossain, the writer of Bangladesh's constitution. As I was driven to the office, I noticed a stream of crimson across the highway – the remnants of a human brain, once alive and pulsating, whose mercy lay in the hands of a speeding stranger. I would later discover that the victim's grieving family was compensated with less than $500 USD. This low value placed on human life troubled me deeply.

Deidre sneered, 'What can you possibly do about it?'

These early confrontations with life's unbalanced scales ignited a fierce resolve within me.

I realised education wasn't merely a path to personal success, but a powerful tool for elevating human worth. By investing in education, we invest in our most valuable asset – human potential. I envisioned it as a catalyst for profound societal change, creating a world where human value is measured by limitless potential, not circumstance. This became my mission: to build an institution offering high-quality, affordable education for all.

Deidre scoffed, 'Noble ideas, but how will you achieve this when you can barely manage yourself?'

Her words stung with truth. During university, anxiety crippled me daily. The voice in my head, Deidre, was getting louder and louder, muffling my own. By 2012, I was in an entry-level legal job. I went to work on the days my anxiety allowed me, but over time, my triumphs grew few and far between.

My corporate position stood in stark contrast to my aspirations. Deidre's voice amplified in the sterile office. I felt no passion for my work at one of Australia's top-tier law firms. The meagre pay and forced laughter only heightened my discontent. I faced a crossroads: continue feigning satisfaction in a pre-determined path, or dare to pursue my true calling?

So, I started arriving at work late, leaving early, and blocking out three-hour timeslots during office hours to play with my friends at Timezone.

During these moments of rebellious escape the words of the stranger I once met resonated deeply: tread carefully – but tread your own path.

Yet, even as I sought refuge in these arcade adventures, I couldn't escape the growing sense of existential dread. In the depths of my darkness, I joined T S Eliot's Prufrock, as we watched as the 'moment of my greatness flicker, the eternal Footman hold my coat, and snicker'.

Deidre whispered, 'This is all you'll ever be.'

It was only through experiencing this profound darkness that I could finally perceive the glimmer of light beyond. As if emerging from a long tunnel, I felt a renewed desire for life and a burning ambition to break free from my corporate shackles.

Instead, I decided to tread the choppy waters of entrepreneurship – a realm few dare to enter. With less than a thousand dollars in my bank account and a head full of dreams, I penned a business plan. I shunned the traditional questions:

What will people say?

That's a very uncertain path. Most businesses fail.

Do you have a plan B?

Instead, I embraced uncertainty with a new found courage.

I was reminded of Ralph Waldo Emerson's words: 'Do not go where the path may lead; go instead where there is no path and leave a trail.' This became my north star as I ventured into the uncharted territory of accessible, premium education.

Reflecting on my first tutoring role at a centre for African refugees, I recalled the children's beaming smiles when solving math problems. These smiles weren't mere expressions; they were triumphs over obstacles, beacons of potential ignited with each new concept grasped. However, my fulfilment was short-lived. I was dismissed because many children from single-mother households couldn't afford the fees. On my last day, as I packed up, unspoken sadness hung in the air. The once-inspiring drawings and charts on the walls now seemed to mock our lost optimism. This experience planted a seed in my mind.

Having been granted the opportunity to attend one of the state's top private schools on a scholarship and complete a law degree that honed my communication skills, I knew I had what it took to offer a premium educational service. More importantly, I recognised the urgent need to make such services accessible and affordable to those who needed them most.

It was 2013, and the tuition industry in my state was relatively underdeveloped. I saw an opportunity, a gap in the market that aligned perfectly with my passion and purpose. Without hesitation, I seized it.

Deidre whispered, 'You're throwing away your law career for this?'

Thus began my journey from corporate law to educational entrepreneurship. I traded pinstripe suits and a high-rise office view for a stack of ten thousand flyers and a winter of door-to-door distribution. The transition was not just a career change but a mission to bridge the educational divide I had witnessed firsthand.

As I trudged through the leafy suburbs of Perth, my mind raced with possibilities. I envisioned a tutoring service that would maintain the high standards of premium education while being accessible to a broader range of students. It would be a place where children from all backgrounds could benefit from quality instruction, and financial constraints wouldn't hinder academic growth. I sought to create what Virginia Woolf might have called 'a room of one's own' for every student – a space where their potential could flourish regardless of their background.

Deidre hissed, 'You're going to fail spectacularly.'

PURPOSE & PASSION

The early days of entrepreneurship were far from glamorous. I felt the pain of financial burden, the inadequacy of unfulfilled expectations, and the anxiety of an unknown future. Most of all, I felt lost. Yet, amidst this cloud of uncertainty, something incredible happened – fear regenerated into faith, extrospection into introspection, pessimism into optimism.

Where others saw challenges, I saw opportunities. My intuition guided me towards distributing those flyers in areas where I knew I could offer a premium service and in neighbourhoods where such services were typically out of reach. I knew the value of what I was offering and refused to undersell it, but I was equally determined to find ways to make education accessible.

One night, as rain poured heavily, I found myself drenched and disoriented, unable to locate my uncle's midnight blue Nissan, which I'd borrowed for this venture. Feeling irritated and helpless, I broke down. Giving up never looked as attractive as at that point. However, I didn't stop. The faces of those refugee children, lighting up with understanding and achievement, kept me going.

After countless evenings of no response, on day twenty-two, I received a call to teach the grandchildren of a prominent Australian family. This call began a journey that would span almost a decade and change my life forever. But more importantly, it was the first step towards realising my vision of democratising premium education.

As my business grew, I never lost sight of my original purpose. While I served some of Western Australia's most affluent families, I also worked tirelessly to develop programs and pricing structures allowing students from less privileged backgrounds to access our services. Every success story, every improved grade and every spark of understanding in a student's eyes reminded me why I had chosen this path.

In hindsight, I see how the principles of the past have guided me in business. On one occasion, as part of an investment finance unit for my commerce degree, all two hundred teams were given fifty thousand dollars play money to invest in the ASX. Our team won, more than doubling our initial investment. I would simmer our success down to three simple rules: make decisions based on undeniable fact, dare to be different and let your intuition guide you. These principles would later become the cornerstone of my business philosophy.

The path of an entrepreneur is paved with challenges and fleeting joys, not unlike any other life journey. Yet, I've come to see time as a precious gift, not a relentless march. Our futures are canvases awaiting our brushstrokes, not predetermined scripts. We are not mere spectators in the theatre of life, but active participants, directors of our own stories.

Marcus Aurelius wisely noted, 'You have power over your mind – not outside events.' This reminder became my compass in the stormy seas of entrepreneurship. It taught me to make choices with vision, to take risks with careful consideration, and to find strength in the face of uncertainty.

It was late one night when I had the realisation to build my business into something much bigger than myself. I knew I had the ideas, the right vision, and the fire in me to burn through the uninhabited bush-land, no matter how thick.

However, I did not have the manpower or countless hours to toil away, creating the basic building blocks of a larger business.

Deidre muttered, 'You're not cut out for this.'

And so, late one night, as the quiet neighbourhood slumbered under a blanket of stars, I found myself at the precipice of creativity. In the still-ness, broken only by the whisper of ideas in my mind, I had the epiphany to build the dream team – an amalgamation of the state's brightest minds, allowing my business to build its next chapter for students, by students.

Today, a business that I spent almost half my lifetime building has a fifteen-year-old second-in-charge. To many, this may seem unabashedly risky. Rather, it is a testament to seeing true value in the individual, once we have cast aside society's 'isms.

Before I knew it, I had managed to swap a five-day work week into a two-day one. Entrepreneurship had granted me the currency of time, and I was galvanised by the possibilities that lay before me. I used this new-found freedom to travel widely – a sojourner in foreign lands.

I visited the high-altitude coffee plantations in Sri Lanka, their earthy, aromatic tendrils weaving through the misty air, composing the very essence of how our world likes to begin its morning. I walked the corridors of Anne Frank's hideaway during the Nazi occupation, my fingers tracing the same walls that once housed dreams and fears alike. In the Maldives, I swam with reef sharks, their sleek bodies cutting through crystal waters, a dance of primal grace and calculated risk.

During one such journey, in Tokyo Station, I found myself lost amongst bustling crowds and unreadable signs. A local man, with whom I did not share a language, spent twelve minutes guiding me to my destination. This selfless act taught me that in business and life, goodwill and kindness pay dividends in incalculable forms.

Thus, entrepreneurship has been rewarding and desirable, granting me freedom. I enjoyed the novelty of being in control of my day, refreshed by the knowledge that I wasn't accountable to anyone: no time sheets, no fussy boss, no deadlines.

But all is not roses in the world of entrepreneurship. It can be a scary, unpredictable ride, not for the faint-hearted. You don't have to work set hours, but sometimes you may feel that you are working all the time. You will meet countless individuals, enlightening and of an assorted variety, but you may feel intensely lonely, especially knowing you will be the only one bearing the brunt of your company's every win and loss.

Deidre sneered, 'See? You're all alone in this.'

My life began in a place where life often ends, amongst one of the poorest countries in the world.

I was born amidst decrepit surrounds, in a nursing home, in Bangladesh. At that time, Bangladesh was one of the poorest nations in the world.

There were no societal privileges, no trust fund and no silver spoon. In its place was: female, Muslim, person of colour, low odds. It seemed to be a life destined to be lived in silent desperation.

By such accounts, I had nothing at all.

By other accounts, I had everything I needed.

Deidre's voice faded, finally silenced.

'Somewhere ages and ages hence: Two roads diverged in a wood, and I –
I took the one less travelled by,
And that has made all the difference.
– The Road Not Taken, Robert Frost

AUTHOR'S NOTE

The journey from that little girl pretending to play piano to the entre-preneur bridging educational divides has been long and challenging, yet immensely rewarding.

To all those facing their own Deidres, remember: your voice matters. Your dreams are valid. And sometimes, the path less travelled makes all the difference.

Morium Khan

Morium Khan's journey from Bangladeshi immigrant to the Founder of Academis Tuition exemplifies the transformative power of education and resilience. Overcoming racism, financial hardship and anxiety during her university years, Khan's experiences fuelled her determination to create positive change.

After earning a scholarship to a top Western Australian school and completing a law and commerce degree at the University of Western Australia, Khan's career took an unexpected turn. In 2011, assisting Nobel Peace Prize Laureate Muhammad Yunus on a high-profile case became a pivotal moment, igniting her passion to drive transformative change through education, much as Yunus had done with microfinance.

In a bold move, Khan traded corporate security for entrepreneurial uncertainty, armed with ten thousand flyers and an unwavering belief in education's power to bridge opportunity gaps. Academis Tuition offers an exceptional tutoring service accessible to students from all backgrounds and embodies Khan's values of educational equity and youth empowerment.

Academis' innovative programs nurture academic excellence, well-being and creativity at affordable rates, reflecting Khan's belief that 'education is the great equaliser'. From ASET preparation and NAPLAN tutoring to ATAR support and university admissions guidance, Academis offers comprehensive educational solutions. Their creative writing and after-school tutoring programs offer peer-to-peer learning and have been meticulously developed by Academis' dream team. The company's impact extends beyond academic achievements to igniting dreams and transforming futures, with initiatives like free trial lessons and scholarship programs ensuring accessibility for all.

Central to Khan's vision is a deep understanding of impending societal changes driven by technology. She advocates for an education system that prepares students for a rapidly evolving job market. 'We're at the precipice of societal transformation,' Khan explains. 'While AI will create new jobs long-term, we face immediate challenges of structural unemployment. Investing in children's education early is crucial to navigating these uncertainties.'

As a female entrepreneur, Khan champions diversity in business. 'We bring unique perspectives, empathetic problem-solving and a commitment to lasting social impact,' she says.

Through Academis, Khan works towards a world where quality education is universally accessible. Her story proves that with determination and clear purpose, one can overcome adversity and pave the way for others to follow.

Why ....?

Petria Cumner

Humans are inquisitive creatures. This is a great trait that helps to keep us alive, learn and grow. There are many times in our life where we ask ourselves *why?* Children ask *why* all the time, it's part of their development, and as adults questions tend to be more; *Why* did things not go right? or perhaps, What is our *why* to the reasoning in the choices we make?

I remember asking my mother an abundance of *why?* questions from a very early age.

Why is the sky blue?

Why do the trees blow in the wind?

Why does it hurt?

Why is the grass green?

Why do you need money to pay for everything?

Why don't people just give it to you?

Why are they so mean?

Why did you get so sick?

Why did you die ...?

Although it still feels like yesterday, a few years have passed now since my best friend and mother passed, but even though I was an adult in my thirties, it was her passing that changed, forever, the direction of what I thought was my career and life path.

Things were great, then suddenly, one by one all the bricks began to fall … until I was at rock bottom. Not just figuratively – literally. I was living a fabulous life in a city high-rise by the river, enjoying life, running my own business in conjunction with a great job, friends and a partner. I had family living in different cities that I'd travel to see on major holidays. I'd love catching up with my five nieces and nephew. Life seemed good again, finally … as it wasn't long before this that I'd escaped a DV situation where I'd been sleeping in my car. I would rush 'home' when it was safe(ish) to have a shower and get ready for work and repeat. Life seemed finally on track again.

It took so much to rebuild, but overnight, it all started to come crashing down. One brick at a time until there was nothing. In less than a year, I went from a good life to no family, no friends, no partner, no job, no home.

If you've ever hit rock bottom, you would be familiar with the myriad of questions that come again. *Why* did it get this way? How …? *Why* am I still here? And then for some of us the darkness falls from questions to statements like, I don't deserve to be here … or worse …

SO, WHAT HAPPENED?

As we get older, we get into the grind and just do. We tend to start to lose our *why*.

I had a varied career in health, corporate and retail management, as well as sales and marketing, until one day, I found myself completely disheartened by it all. I was purely working for power and money. I had achieved the highest position each time. I was successful. But I was unfulfilled. I had also suffered from burnout, depression, anxiety, workplace bullying and sexual assault where my employer did nothing. I no longer wanted to be a part of the egos and events I witnessed happening to me and around me.

FEEL THE FEAR AND DO IT ANYWAY

The easy thing would have been to get a new corporate career with all the experience I'd gained over the years, but in my late twenties, I decided to go back to study and chase my creative lifelong passion for interior design. I dropped all my ranks and became a rookie travel agent to put myself through design school. It was bloody hard, but before I knew it, I had worked hard to have my own interior design business working on multimillion-dollar homes locally and abroad. Homes for everyday families to TV personalities and sporting stars.

MUM GOT SICK ...

I'd never been a carer, other than looking after the animals on the farm where I grew up. I would diligently and lovingly nurse back to health any that were sick or injured, but I had never had the slightest desire to become a nurse. Although I admired them for their work, I would look at what nurses had to do and knew it was something I never wanted.

However, when she got sick, looking after Mum was all I wanted to do. Even though she had worked full-time, she'd devoted her life to her children. Every fall, every heartbreak, those moments of self-doubt, every time I moved house (there were many!), she was there to help. No question, no complaining or excuses. She was always there. It was our turn as her children to help her.

Without hesitation, I put my life on pause; Mum needed me. It was the easiest decision of my life and the hardest thing I've ever had to do. However, I would not have missed that time with my mother, nor the opportunity to help her. I adored my mother and fiercely protected her when she could no longer care for herself. In hospital, she and the nurses relied on me being there to understand what she was going through and how to treat her. My previous studies and work within health and medicine, along with my personal experience, assisted me in doing this. She had lost the ability to speak for herself. I knew her micro expressions of pain. My mum, the strongest woman I had known, had become visibly terrified when I left her side for an hour to do washing and walk my dog, Truffles. Inside, I was also terrified …

In a period of fourteen months, I pulled out of the biggest design job of my career to move cities and become my mother's carer. While at her hospital bedside, my partner, not being able to handle the situation, told me over the phone that he 'couldn't do our relationship anymore', moments after I'd informed him that the doctor had been in to say it was time to say goodbye to Mum. My friends had their own lives in other cities.

… AND THEN, MY MOTHER DIED …

I felt so alone, with no-one to share my deepest thoughts and concerns with.

Two out of my three siblings were not handling their grief and were viciously abusing me daily. They even said I would never see their children again – my nieces and nephew, my godchildren.

Mum and I both had applied to volunteer for the Commonwealth Games together before she fell very ill. After she passed, I received confirmation that I was selected but it wasn't for the role I had gone for. It was hers. I was broken and needed to grieve. It was the last thing I wanted to do. But I knew I had to help myself.

I volunteered for the Commonwealth Games.

I started, and ended, a new relationship with Ben, an old high school friend.

And because I had relocated to look after Mum, when the estate sold her home in a flash, I was left homeless.

I had given up on the world and did not want to live anymore.

Then I found out I was pregnant. This tiny little being ignited my desire to survive and sparked my fight to live.

Life will knock us down. It's our choice if we choose to get back up or not.

My life had completely changed forever. Nothing was the same. After such a turbulent and traumatic time, I had completely lost myself, my family and my people. I had to find my purpose and passion again.

To say I was struggling is a severe understatement. Under intense stress, alone, I was growing a baby inside of me, I was trying to deal with mum's estate. I was living in a friend's basement trying to find a safe home for me and my soon-to-arrive baby. I'd been keeping my pregnancy a secret, fearful that the abuse from my two siblings would become more vicious. I had not had time to grieve.

In a very short space of time, I had gone through a huge evolutionary experience. I was a changed woman forever. I had lost my zest, my spark. My happy smile, that people regularly commented on, was gone. I had gone from always smiling, to not knowing how to smile anymore.

REBIRTH

My baby boy changed all of that. This bundle of purity helped me, when I believed there was nothing that could help me.

Ben and I were back together, and we moved cities during the pandemic. At the start of lockdown, when we couldn't find a removalist, we had to move ourselves in seventeen car-loads with help from my supportive brother, Mark, and new dear friend, Sue.

It was during this time I saw something that would not only change my life but would transform all three of our lives … forever.

Next to our six-month-old son was a mountain of plastic water bottles. We had created a huge pile of bottles to recycle. Previously I would simply drop them into the recycling bin or collection for Containers for Change. I'd done my bit. Gone!

But this day was different. As I saw them beside my very small child, it hit me like a ton of bricks. I realised we were only one small family in this world, and this mountain was only a couple of days' worth of our contribution to the global plastic problem; a problem that doesn't degrade but hangs around for hundreds of years.

The problem that our son and his generation was set to inherit from all of us.

This was not the type of 'inheritance' I wanted to leave behind. I did not want to contribute to this any longer. We had reusable water bottles at home, but with a new baby and a dog, we needed to be hands-free. We needed to be able to carry the bottles somehow so they were convenient and left our hands available. We decided to create a product to solve this.

Suddenly, with our daily use of our creation, public interest spiked. Orders started coming in. Making bottle harnesses became an unexpected hobby. I was researching night and day about all kinds of environmental problems, specifically, the global plastic problem. My mind was exploding at how little was being done by governments to prevent the problem from becoming astronomically out of control. In fact, they were facilitating the problem, supporting large corporations and their terrible environmental contribution.

My interest and passion began growing in this area. Once I started to look below the surface and really learn about things, I couldn't unsee them. As a protective new parent, when you feel so strongly about something, you simply have to do something about it.

I am only one person, but I felt I had to do something to instigate change. I'm not the type of personality to sit back and complain that someone isn't doing something and not do anything myself. My son and his friends' generation was going to suffer and we couldn't wait for the government to make changes. This hobby was going to grow into something much bigger.

A LEGACY IS BORN

Mum never got to meet her grandson whom she would have loved and adored, cherished and spoilt. Neither of them got to experience joy and love from each other. Mum knew how much I wanted to start my own family but after countless miscarriages, tumour, endometriosis and a start and fail to an IVF journey, I had all but given up. It was only months after Mum's passing that my body finally held onto a pregnancy.

Life is too short not to have faith and take risks.

After a huge deliberation, I decided to take a massive risk. I used a chunk of mum's inheritance to start a business for Stirling's future. Instead of putting the money into a house, I opted to invest it, not in the traditional sense, but into a business with heart and one that advocates for change. This leap of faith uncovered a passion with purpose I had never felt before.

All of those different career paths I had taken were not pointless. I'd, in fact, been banking a wealth of knowledge and priceless experience. I put my vast experience to work. Not for a corporation this time but for myself, the next generation and the planet.

This was a chance to help educate and instigate change. Offer solutions for a better tomorrow. I wanted my son, and his own children, to witness the beauty of nature and pick up seashells from the beach; not to witness the destruction of mankind's hand on nature, picking up micro plastics, plastic bottles and creatures that have died from our pollution.

'An idea isn't worth that much. It's the execution of the idea that has value.'
– Joel Spolsky

I had a vision. After a year of dedicated research, I decided to create an eco-ecommerce business. It was important to me to keep a minimal footprint, be Australian-made and use Australian supplies as much as possible. I started to build the website myself. Long hours night and day, often finishing in the early hours of the morning. Stirling was a baby. Many people just didn't understand my drive or purpose, urging me to get a job packing shelves or teaching swim classes to get me out of the house. They didn't care for the vision I was working towards and wanted to see me earning any sort of income immediately. Again, that would have been the easy thing to do. Instead, I knuckled down harder. I had to make this work. It was Mum's legacy for Stirling's future.

Even my partner struggled to believe it would work. I almost gave up. What's the point? No-one believes in me anymore. *Why* am I doing this? I am putting so much time and energy into this. Minimal sleep. Stirling wasn't sleeping well, and I hadn't had a break or time to myself in I couldn't remember how long … but in my darkest moments, halfway through a box of tissues, a little voice came from out of nowhere; *Keep going! Mum would have believed in you.* You can do this! I'd put the tissues down, pick myself up, refocus and get back into it.

I launched the website in time for Plastic Free July – 1 July 2022. Suddenly people got it!

There was amazement in what I had created and the pieces Ben and I had made.

Our first sales started coming in just minutes after launching. Within a month there were plans to take the business globally. Investors and buyers were calling. Overseas businesses wanted to start manufacturing our plastic-free lifestyle products for us at a fraction of the cost, which of course I had to decline. It was against *why* the business was born and what it was trying to achieve.

In three months, we won our first award, solidifying our commitment.

I was already invested through *why* I was doing this; change needed to happen in the world, the future for my son, the passion, mum's legacy, but this validation reinforced that others also believed. It wasn't just one person's pipe dream. Our commitment to making a difference and striving for a better world for our children was going to grow.

My goal is to encourage people to think innovatively. Encourage them to view their lifestyle choices from a fresh perspective; instead of accepting things at face value as suggested by marketing departments. The aim is to raise awareness, so individuals pause and question: *Why?* *Why* do we follow these practices and what impact do they have on the planet? Are there other options available?

Life can throw unexpected curveballs that can alter everything in an instant. However, it is our reactions and decisions that shape our path. As challenging as it may be at times, embracing change to continue to grow is crucial for navigating through these moments.

As I have experienced a few hard hands in life and evolved, my *whys* have also evolved. *Why* do I do what I do each day? For the first time in my life, I don't only answer this with a passion, but I now answer with clarity and a heart full of purpose.

When you can answer that for yourself, you know you are on the right path.

Petria Cumner

Petria Cumner's life path has been an intricate tapestry, weaving together diverse experiences that have shaped her unique journey. Her story is a testament to her unwavering determination and the resilience that has carried her through. From her humble beginnings on a farm to her foray into the fashion industry at a young age, Petria's talents have propelled her into a multifaceted career. Her journey encompasses years of study and the realms of pharmacy, natural medicine, marketing and advertising, including roles at Australia's leading media companies, Queensland marketing manager for an international real estate company, resident decorator for a major furniture chain, to establishing two businesses, Petria Liana Interior Design and sustainable award-winning brand, Stirling & Truffles.

Yet, amidst this success, Petria experienced the darkest shadows of life, grappling with domestic violence, trauma, PTSD, depression and anxiety. She emerged as a resilient warrior, channelling her energies into creating her art and interior design business. Petria's entrepreneurial spirit gave birth to Petria Liana Interior Design. Her dedication, attention to detail and expertise garnered recognition, attracting global clientele from Australian celebrities and sporting stars to international businesses. Her designs have left an indelible mark on head offices, shopping centres, clinical spaces and homes. Her influence extends beyond borders, with her work reaching the Middle East, South East Asia, and the UK. Petria's skills were evident in transforming spaces into works of art that resonated with the personalities of her clients.

Yet her true calling awaited her. Inspired by the birth of her son, Petria's enduring spirit led her to found Stirling & Truffles, a sustainable lifestyle brand and consulting business. Her tireless study and commitment to sustainability have propelled the business into the limelight now multi-award-winning, including global accolades such as the prestigious Women Changing the World Awards in London – presented by The Duchess of York, where she won bronze for Woman in Sustainability. These acknowledgements speak volumes about her steadfast commitment to making an eco-conscious impact. Through Stirling & Truffles, Petria has embarked on a mission to reduce single-use plastic waste not only through the products produced by Stirling & Truffles but also in services, assisting businesses transition to more sustainable practices, event speaking and advocating for legislative change. She was also instrumental as the sustainability partner in making the inaugural Toowoomba Fashion Festival the first sustainably run fashion event in Australia where she and partner Ben also showcased their first sustainable runway collection.

Petria's busy schedule finds balance in her personal life, where she resides in Queensland, enjoying the company of her partner Ben, their young son, Stirling, Truffles the dooxiepoo, mini dachshund Louis and chickens.

The story of Petria Cumner unfolds with a blend of determination, creativity and a profound commitment to making a lasting impact on the world through her sustainable endeavours. Her journey is a testament to the transformative power of passion and perseverance.

Words Without Action Are Only Noise

Sarah Barnbrook

In the intricate dance of balancing success in business, volunteering and motherhood, fulfilment lies not solely on our external achievements, but through the cultivation of inner strength. As women, our journey towards fulfilment is imbued with the resilience, courage and compassion that resides within us, guiding us through the highs and lows of our multifaceted roles. In this chapter, I'd like to delve deeper into the significance of inner strength in our pursuit of fulfilment, intertwining curiosity, experimentation, reflection, giving back, seeking inspiration, and, most importantly, practicing self-compassion and embracing the journey.

Sometimes, I've felt like I'm lost at sea in a small rowboat, uncertain what direction would lead me back to shore. When significant challenges have crashed into me, like giant waves swelling around me, I have calmed the storm within myself to find the courage to navigate the treacherous water pouring into my boat.

I had just arrived at the hospital, nine months pregnant, listening to a nurse leave a voicemail for me, about something life-threatening they needed urgent consent for. I remember thinking at that moment how awful it would be to receive that kind of voicemail, not knowing that message was being left for me. I'll never forget the tone of voice the nurse used, full of compassion and strength. Her words painted the picture of profound urgency, without the panic that most of the public would use when discussing something so serious.

Back then, I didn't carry a mobile phone with me. I had just started maternity leave, clocking off at 5pm on Friday. You see, I wasn't at the hospital for myself; I was there to visit my husband at the time, who was a lot sicker than we had initially realised, as the voicemail spelled out when I got home hours later to find it waiting for me. By the time I got to listen to that voicemail, my entire world had already been turned upside-down.

The next two weeks were a blur of life support, last rites, thousands of kilometres of driving to the hospital and back and several surgeries, including my own C-section and the introduction of my third child into the world. I named her after light, as she was my beacon during the darkest days – when there weren't enough buckets to empty my boat from all the water crashing in. Children have that way about them; saving us when we are the ones who are supposed to be protecting them, giving us purpose and focus.

I strongly believe in miracles; especially those against all odds. Despite everything stacked against him, a few celestial favours were cashed in, and he managed to pull through. However, his formal diagnosis is *incomplete quadriplegia* from critical illness polyneuropathy due to severe sepsis. The journey ahead for him proved to be long and arduous; difficult for everyone in the family, full of advocacy, self-efficacy, challenges, tears, distance and eighteen months before we could all live together again as a young family. He could write an entire book on his experiences, and perhaps he should.

Through many of my experiences over the last decade, supporting someone with a profound physical disability, I came to understand that I wasn't just in a rowboat – I was in a lifeboat. I had already escaped the shipwreck and could charter my course. I did that by volunteering, not just as a carer, partner or mother, but as an opportunity *to be Sarah,* to just be myself. I signed up for the school council, local agricultural shows and the Country Women's Association of Victoria Inc. Helping others has always helped me, sharing my strength and shining my light for others in the dark.

EMBRACING CURIOSITY: A JOURNEY OF SELF-DISCOVERY

Curiosity is the spark that ignites our quest for fulfilment, prompting us to explore the depths of our passions, purpose and potential. Our curiosity propels us to venture beyond the confines of convention, to seek out new ideas, opportunities and perspectives that challenge the status quo and expand our horizons. In our volunteer roles, curiosity compels us to delve into the complexities of social issues to confront injustice and inequality with a spirit of inquiry and empathy. As mothers, curiosity invites us to embark on a journey of discovery alongside our children, to nurture their curiosity, creativity and wonder as they navigate the world with fresh eyes and open hearts.

EXPERIMENTING WITH NEW EXPERIENCES: EMBRACING GROWTH AND RESILIENCE

Experimentation is the crucible in which our inner strength is forged as we navigate the uncertainties and challenges of stepping outside our comfort zones. Experimentation empowers us to innovate, adapt and evolve in the face of adversity, to turn setbacks into opportunities for growth and resolute resilience. As a volunteer, experimentation allows us to test the boundaries of our compassion and commitment and explore new ways of making a meaningful impact in our communities and beyond. Experimenting as a mother invites us to embrace the unpredictability of parenthood and navigate the ebbs and flows of caregiving with grace, flexibility and unwavering love.

REFLECTING ON PAST EXPERIENCES: MINING WISDOM FROM WITHIN

Reflection is the wellspring of our inner strength as we draw upon the wisdom, insights and lessons learned from our past experiences. Reflecting on business success enables us to glean valuable insights into our strengths, weaknesses and areas for growth to chart a course towards success rooted in self-awareness and authenticity. In our volunteer work, reflection deepens our understanding of our impact on others, illuminating the ripple effects of our actions and contributions to the world. As mothers, reflection allows us to savour the moments of joy, connection and growth that enrich our journey of motherhood and to honour the challenges and triumphs that shape us as caregivers, nurturers and role models.

GIVING BACK: NURTURING COMPASSION AND CONNECTION

Giving back embodies our inner strength as we extend our compassion, empathy and resources to uplift those in need and create positive change in the world. Giving back empowers us to leverage our influence and resources for the greater good and to use our successful business platform to amplify the voices of the marginalised and underserved. In volunteering, giving back fosters a sense of connection and community as we join forces with like-minded individuals and organisations to address pressing social issues and advance the common good. As mothers, giving back instils in our children a sense of empathy, kindness and social responsibility, nurturing a legacy of compassion and service that transcends generations.

SEEKING INSPIRATION FROM OTHERS: FOSTERING GROWTH AND EMPOWERMENT

Seeking inspiration from others is an act of courage and humility as we open ourselves to the wisdom, guidance and support of those who have walked the path before us. Seeking inspiration from other women in business empowers us to learn from the triumphs and tribulations of trailblazers and mentors to glean valuable insights and strategies for success. Seeking inspiration through volunteering ignites a fire as we connect with individuals and organisations that embody the values and aspirations we hold dear. As mothers, seeking inspiration nourishes our souls as we draw strength and encouragement from the stories of resilience, love and sacrifice that illuminate the journey of motherhood.

PRACTICING SELF-COMPASSION: CULTIVATING GRACE AND RESILIENCE

Practicing self-compassion is an act of radical self-love and acceptance as we embrace our imperfections, vulnerabilities and humanity with kindness and grace. As businesswomen, self-compassion enables us to navigate the pressures and expectations of leadership with resilience and authenticity, honouring our needs and wellbeing amidst the demands of our professional lives.

As volunteers, practising self-compassion fosters a sense of balance and perspective as we prioritise our mental, emotional and physical health in service of our commitment to others. As a mum, practicing self-compassion can empower us to embrace the messy, beautiful journey of parenthood with grace and levelheadedness, forgive ourselves for our mistakes and shortcomings and celebrate the moments of joy, connection and growth that define our role as caregivers and nurturers.

EMBRACING THE JOURNEY: FINDING PEACE AND PURPOSE IN EVERY STEP

Ultimately, our journey towards fulfilment is a testament to the strength, resilience and grace that reside within us, guiding us through the complexities and uncertainties of life with courage, compassion and authenticity. Let us embrace the journey with open hearts and open minds, celebrating the moments of joy, connection and growth illuminating our path and finding peace and purpose in every step we take.

Sarah Barnbrook

Sarah Barnbrook has dedicated her life to empowering the vulnerable, nurturing communities, and creating spaces where everyone can find belonging. From a young age, she volunteered at her local women's shelter, instilling a deep commitment to compassion and empathy – values that have guided her ever since.

Throughout her life, Sarah has been actively involved in numerous community organizations, continually seeking ways to contribute and make a difference. However, over ten years ago, she found her true home in the Country Women's Association of Victoria Inc. (CWA). Since joining the CWA, Sarah's dedication and leadership have seen her rise to the role of deputy state president, with the honour of becoming state president next year. She has been pivotal in respecting the Association's history while driving initiatives that pave the way for future generations.

The CWA is renowned for its unwavering support of vulnerable women and children, providing essential resources and advocacy that make a tangible difference in their lives. The Association's efforts extend to lobbying for policy changes that protect and empower those in need, demonstrating a commitment to social justice and community welfare that aligns deeply with Sarah's values.

In addition, Sarah is the founder of Away from Keyboard (AFK) Inc., a not-for-profit organisation that encourages children to disconnect from screens and engage in meaningful, in-person interactions. This initiative is a testament to her commitment to fostering social connectedness and supporting community well-being.

Sarah's entrepreneurial spirit shines through in the success of her retail shop, Board Games and Battlegrounds, a hub for gaming enthusiasts and a place that offers job opportunities for a neurodiverse workforce. It has become a cherished community space where everyone feels welcome.

At the core of Sarah's approach to life and leadership is a belief in the power of vulnerability and authenticity. Sarah advocates for leading with kindness, knowing that it is through kindness that we build stronger, more resilient communities.

Balancing her professional endeavours, Sarah remains a devoted live-in carer for her family, including a family member who is an incomplete quadriplegic. She supports her three neurodivergent children through the unique challenges they face, from navigating the complexities of the educational system to advocating for their individual needs in a world that often doesn't understand them. Sarah's commitment to her children involves being their strongest advocate and providing them with a nurturing environment where they can thrive, celebrate their differences, and grow into resilient individuals.

Her experience has only strengthened her resolve to be a voice for those who cannot always speak for themselves. Sarah's journey with her family has deepened her understanding of the diverse needs of living with a disability and the importance of tailored support systems that empower rather than limit them.

As a role model and friend, Sarah seamlessly blends her professional responsibilities with her mission of kindness and support. Through her public service, leadership in community organisations, growing business, and personal experiences as a carer, Sarah embodies the power of compassion and the significant impact one person can make.

Like A Scene Out Of *Fawlty Towers* Or *The Truman Show*

Sarah MacRae

S ome days, that's just how I feel …

My early experiences were far from conventional, beginning with a significant family move from our hometown of Moss Vale to Brooklyn, an outer suburb of Sydney, and eventually to Dangar Island – a unique and challenging environment, accessible only by boat. This new way of life, in a community of only around three hundred people, taught me early lessons in resilience and adaptability, learning to navigate boats and tides, as well as handling the perils of being stuck on mud flats during changing tides.

Our family business was the epicentre of my early life education. Much like a scene from *Fawlty Towers,* it was managed amid the chaos of four wild children and the constant hum of sibling arguments. We were all integrated into the daily operations, providing me with a hands-on experience of what it takes to run a business, seven days a week. These formative years were pivotal, imbuing me with a deep understanding of commitment and the rigorous demands of business management.

The shop was not just a place of commerce but where I learned the value of hard work and the realities of business ownership.

LESSONS LEARNED FROM EARLY LEADERSHIP

When my parents separated, the responsibility of managing the shop fell to me, while my father worked elsewhere to keep our financial ship afloat. This period forced me to mature rapidly, acquiring skills that would lay the groundwork for my future endeavours. Running the shop taught me the importance of having a strong structure and a dedicated team. I learned firsthand how quickly things can unravel without these elements, as I juggled long hours and sacrificed my social life to keep the business going. These experiences taught me how fragile business can be and the relentless commitment required to sustain it.

Although this phase of my life was filled with challenges, it was instrumental in shaping my approach to leadership and entrepreneurship. The skills I developed during this time – problem-solving, team management and resilience – became foundational elements in my career, influencing how I would later handle complex projects and lead my own initiatives.

TRANSITION TO BROADER HORIZONS

Moving to Peat Island in my late teens became a significant chapter in my life, one where I was able to diversify my skills, working in various capacities that broadened my understanding of community needs and organisational management.

When I moved there, Peat Island was an established medical facility, catering for people with disabilities and mental illness. I was so naive, unknowing that a world like that existed in our society, yet it was in this unlikely refuge, among the island's secluded residents and eclectic staff, that I finally found my tribe. I had stumbled upon a sense of belonging that had eluded me all my life.

Throughout many years working on the island, I explored a variety of roles, each station teaching me something about myself, along with skills that would prove to be invaluable in my own business. From the steam-filled laundry room to the organised chaos of the kitchen and the hands-on maintenance crew, each assignment added something new to my ever-expanding professional skills. It was my time in nursing administration, though, that helped me build my confidence and underpin the many skills I use now in my own business.

I loved my work on Peat Island, as I was able to support others, and for the first time, I had a sense of passion and purpose, an idea of where I fitted into the world.

When the decision was made to decommission Peat Island, I worked closely with the transition team, ensuring that our residents were integrated into the community with dignity and care.

LEGACY AND FUTURE ASPIRATIONS

With a heart brimming with love, my greatest achievement is being the proud mother of two strong-willed and resilient, beautiful girls; the two Rael loves of my life.

Being an eighties baby, as well as a survivor of child sexual abuse, I was often considered 'a ratbag' and a 'troubled teen'. If I'd been born into this generation, I may have had a diagnosis and been considered differently – who knows? I transitioned into my adult life as a wild, eighteen-year-old mum to my first daughter, Emily.

As a young mum, I provided for my family as a single independent parent, navigating the complexities of shift work and intermittent child care on Peat Island to make ends meet. Emily grew up with the *unhealed* version of me. She has experienced my mistakes which have caused her some pain, but it has also helped her grow into one of the strongest and most resilient women I know. She is a powerhouse and passionate advocate for people with disabilities, as well as an amazing disability support worker. Above all, she has supported me to become a better version of myself.

I truly know she was sent to me, as young as I was, to save me from heading down a dark road where I would likely not have found my way home to experience life to the fullest.

My second daughter, Macie, has taught me so much in the short eight years she has been on Earth. With the challenges of complex trauma and special needs with her disabilities, I am fighting for her every day. I am blessed not to have lost her in accidents that have occurred within education, health and specialised support services, which seem to be trying to keep her in the very system which has so far failed us.

All of this is the fuel that keeps my fire burning, to get up after being knocked down time and time again. Balancing the joys and hurdles of parenthood, and being a mumpreneuer, I embrace each moment with grace and courage. Dedicating myself to nurturing and caring for my daughters. My commitment to their happiness and wellbeing reflects my resolute dedication to family.

And this has also supported my development into my purpose; not just to create a safe and satisfying life for my own family, but to make change for others by being a part of a community and a business owner who can provide a service that will push for change, through this ship I now lead with my crew, my tribe, my community.

FOUNDING A VISIONARY ORGANISATION

Beyond motherhood, my journey into business ownership has been punctuated by notable accolades (including awards such as 'Highly Commended Carer of the Year' and 'Employer of the Year') but also profound setbacks. Despite the hardships, enduring personal trials and confronting societal barriers, my spirit remains unbroken. My organisation, 24/7 Care, now stands as a testament to my commitment to excellence and compassion, reflecting my belief in the transformative power of caregiving.

The closure of Peat Island was not an end but a beginning. It fuelled within me a desire to create an inclusive space that transcended traditional care models.

The culmination of my purpose, passion and professional experiences inspired me to establish an organisation that mirrored the values I had come to uphold – community, inclusivity and resilience. My vision was to create a welcoming space offering more than just services; I wanted to build a community hub that fostered support and opportunity for those who had been marginalised by society.

This organisation was not just a continuation of my business journey, but a reflection of my personal evolution, from a young girl on Dangar Island, learning the ropes of a challenging family business, to a leader passionate about making a difference in the lives of others. My unique upbringing and the diverse roles I embraced over the years equipped me with a rare perspective on the power of a supportive community and the impact of compassionate leadership.

As a passionate advocate for individuals with disabilities, I've dedicated myself to raising awareness and promoting inclusivity. Through my advocacy work, I strive to foster a more supportive and inclusive community for individuals of all abilities, ensuring they are valued members of society.

Looking back, I'm inspired by the impact my work has had on others. It's a reminder that with passion, resilience and determination, anything is possible – even when the odds seem stacked against you.

Sarah MacRae

H i, I would like to introduce myself. My name is Sarah MacRae, the eldest of four siblings, born and raised amidst the picturesque freezing landscapes of the Southern Highlands. My journey has been one of resilience and transformation, despite facing personal tragedy, such as the loss of my youngest brother, Keith. Throughout these challenges, I've achieved milestones that I am genuinely honoured to share.

I'm a proud mother to two amazing girls, Emily-May and Macie, who are the center of my universe. My greatest achievements are undoubtedly my children, and I am deeply grateful for the unwavering love and support from my incredible partner, Rael. Rekindling our high school romance twenty-five years later, Rael has been my soulmate and my strength. My family and close-knit tribe mean everything to me, especially my youngest daughter, who, at just eight years old, faces challenges with ASD and complex trauma. Her resilience is awe-inspiring and motivates me to keep going through life's ups and downs.

Balancing motherhood and running my own business isn't easy, but it's a challenge I embrace with grace and courage. My dedication to my daughters' wellbeing drives me forward, pushing me to overcome obstacles and seize every moment.

Twenty-seven years of experience in the disability field, advocacy is in my blood. It's a privilege to speak up for those who often don't have a voice of their own. I am on a mission to raise awareness and promote inclusivity. Everyone deserves to be valued and empowered, regardless of their abilities.

I have a relentless drive that stems from transforming my emotions of anger and hurt into a powerful force for creating and achieving societal change or nurturing my daughters' growth, I give it my all. Each day is an opportunity to make a positive impact .

In my story, you'll find a blend of resilience, compassion and determination. I'm here to leave my mark, to inspire others to embrace their journey and to make a difference in the world. With every step I take, I'm reminded that the greatest achievements often come from the toughest challenges.

Beyond my roles as a mother and advocate, I've had the privilege of being involved in various community initiatives. Giving back to the community is a core value I hold dear. I've seen firsthand the power of collective action and its positive impact on the world around us.

Looking ahead, I'm excited to continue my journey of growth and impact. Whether expanding, growing my business or simply being there for my family, I'm committed to making the most of every opportunity. As I navigate the road ahead, I'm grateful for the love and support of those who have been by my side every step of the way.

With love in my heart and fire in my soul, I'm ready to take on whatever challenges lie ahead continuing making a positive impact in the lives of others.

I See You

Dr Sascha Kowalenko

My dear entrepreneurial mother-in-arms,
I see you.

I see you and your big, beautiful heart, mind and brain.

I see your deep, deep desire to have a big impact in the world.

I see you wanting to do life differently – so very differently and so very desperately – because you know that your wellbeing and the wellbeing of your children, your relationships, your family and your community – and the future of generations to follow – *depends* on you doing life differently.

I see your crystal-clear vision of the life you want to live. A life defined by freedom – pure and simple. Freedom to choose ... to slow down, to speed up, to go this way or that ... on your terms.

I see you acknowledging the privilege of your position and you knowing that it is your duty to harness the power of your privilege for those who are not so lucky.

I see all of the above as your personal 'why' for your step (or leap) into entrepreneurship and the stewarding of your own ship. It is why you contemplated entrepreneurship, as opposed to the relative (and supposed) safety and security of other working-mother options; options that have no doubt also fuelled your drive towards entrepreneurship. Options that without any fault of your own, and despite your very best efforts, inevitably and invariably have led you down a path of guilt, shame, self-sacrifice and physical and emotional burnout that has no end.

I see you now at a crossroads. That crossroads might come in the form of dipping your toes into entrepreneurship, whilst still holding on to the edge of the pool. It might be that you are contemplating diving all the way in (likely into the deep end) and leaving behind some degree of security and stability of past income source, career pathway or even relationship. I might now find you knee-deep in the messy middle of your entrepreneurial journey where you are contemplating throwing in the towel, on more days than not.

I see you and I want you to know you are not alone.

Wherever you may be on your entrepreneurial journey (contemplating, dreaming, sustaining, growing and scaling), I want you to know you have ALL that it takes to have the life you so deeply desire, knowing that your business is simply one of the conduits to making that happen.

I know you possess within you all that you require to succeed.

I also know you don't always see or feel like this.

And often this isn't your fault, either. The pervasive and, often unidentified, myth of the entrepreneurial unicorn – the belief that successful entrepreneurs are born with innate talents and destined for greatness – can weigh heavily on your shoulders, leaving you feeling as though you must measure up to an impossible, possibly indefinable, standard.

But I'm here to tell you you are more than enough – just as you are. And I'm not saying that in the toxic positivity kind of way of 'you've got this'.

You, as a woman and a mother, first and foremost, bring to the entrepreneurial table a wealth of experiences, skills and insights, uniquely positioning you for success in the entrepreneurial world.

Your journey through motherhood has equipped you with a diverse set of core skills; emotional intelligence, resilience, problem-solving, time management, adaptability and communication. These skills are not just invaluable assets in entrepreneurship, they are what underpin entrepreneurial success.

Your skills are not the issue. The issue is that these skills are 'hidden in plain sight'. Or perhaps, you are pigeon-holing your skills in one domain of your life, most likely, motherhood and/or your former career, rather than seeing these skills as universal skills that transcend all aspects of your life, particularly the world of entrepreneurship.

What does it mean to be *hidden in plain sight?* This concept speaks to recognising the inherent skills, talents and experiences that may go unnoticed or underappreciated in our day-to-day lives. These hidden strengths are often overshadowed by the demands of our roles and responsibilities, yet they hold the key to unlocking our full potential and achieving our goals.

By bringing these hidden strengths to light, you can harness their power to ensure you keep on going when you feel like giving up.

This is truly the only 'thing' that counts in entrepreneurial success.

You are smart and you are resourceful. You are all the things that I'm going to shine some light on in a moment. The only factor that will determine whether you succeed or fail is whether you give up or keep going.

So let me shine some light on what lies hidden, how you can harness this skill and power in entrepreneurship and what to do if you feel a little shaky and in need of shoring up the foundations of this skill domain.

YOUR EMOTIONAL INTELLIGENCE IS NEXT-LEVEL

As a mother, you have honed the ability to empathise, communicate effectively and manage emotions in challenging situations. These skills are the foundation of meaningful relationships, with your children, your family and your community, and they are equally essential for building strong connections with your customers, employees and stakeholders in business. And emotional intelligence is not just foundational to your ability to navigate tricky situations with others, it is critical to the other much-talked about entrepreneurial success variable; the ability to tolerate discomfort (take risks, feel-fear-and-do-it-anyway kind of slogans).

EXAMPLES OF HIDDEN SKILLS

Remember the countless times you comforted your child through tears, deciphered their needs without words or celebrated their victories with genuine joy? That's emotional intelligence and empathy in action.

Think about the times you navigated delicate conversations with your partner, explained complex concepts to your children or negotiated with your toddler over bedtime. Each interaction was an opportunity to refine your communication skills, grounded in your ability to understand their experience and shape your response accordingly.

Recall the times you adjusted your parenting approach to meet the changing needs of your children or navigated unexpected challenges with flexibility and grace (adaptability).

DEVELOPMENT STRATEGIES

Take time to truly listen to your customers, employees and stakeholders. Ask open-ended questions, reflect on their perspectives and validate their feelings, just as you do with your children.

Invite constructive feedback from trusted mentors, colleagues or peers. Use their insights to refine your communication style and enhance your emotional intelligence.

RESILIENCE IS YOUR SUPERPOWER

Motherhood is a journey filled with ups and downs, triumphs and challenges. You have faced adversity head-on, weathered storms and emerged stronger and more resilient than ever before. You know how to bounce back from setbacks, adapt to change and persevere through difficult times. Let this resilience be your guiding light as you navigate the uncertainties of entrepreneurship, knowing that every obstacle you overcome brings you one step closer to your goals.

EXAMPLES OF HIDDEN SKILLS

As painful as it might be, remember the days and nights you showed up for your children and your family, literally running on empty (little or no sleep, little or no respite from demands) ... the physical pain of pregnancy, childbirth, establishing breastfeeding. These are all examples of experiences that most likely brought incredible physical discomfort and emotional distress. Did you give up? I know that you didn't. You kept going. You pushed through the pain, the discomfort, the uncertainty.

DEVELOPMENT STRATEGIES

View challenges in your entrepreneurial enterprise as opportunities for growth and learning. Dig deep into the resilience you demonstrate through motherhood and apply that grit and determination to business. Think to yourself, *I will approach this problem, this challenge, this feeling of discomfort/fear/being out of control, just like I do any issue with my children and my family. I will think it through. I will problem-solve. I will work it out.*

Surround yourself with mentors, peers or fellow entrepreneurs who can offer guidance, encouragement and perspective during challenging times.

YOUR PROBLEM-SOLVING SKILL IS SECOND-TO-NONE

As a mother, you are the ultimate problem-solver, constantly finding creative solutions to everyday challenges. Whether it's soothing a crying baby, managing household chores or navigating the complexities of parenting, you approach each problem with determination and ingenuity. In business, this same resourcefulness and creativity will serve you well, as you tackle obstacles, seize opportunities and drive innovation.

EXAMPLES OF HIDDEN SKILLS

Consider the times you improvised with limited resources to create engaging activities for your children, prepared meals from whatever ingredients were available or found innovative solutions to household dilemmas (resourcefulness).

Reflect on the decisions you made to balance competing priorities, allocate resources effectively, and anticipate future needs or challenges (strategic thinking).

DEVELOPMENT STRATEGIES

Stay curious and open-minded, seeking inspiration and new ideas from diverse sources. Explore different perspectives, industries and approaches to problem-solving – intentionally. Don't beat yourself up if the answer isn't immediately forthcoming; remember you have what it takes to find the solution.

Challenge yourself to think outside the box and explore unconventional solutions to familiar problems. Engage in brainstorming sessions, collaborate with others and embrace experimentation.

YOU MANAGE TIME (AND DO NOT ALLOW TIME TO MANAGE YOU)

Motherhood demands a constant juggling act, where you must balance the needs of your family with the demands of everyday life. You have mastered the art of prioritisation, delegation and time management, maximising your productivity and efficiency to make the most of every moment. In entrepreneurship, these skills will be your secret weapon, helping you stay focused, organised and on track as you pursue your business goals.

EXAMPLES OF HIDDEN SKILLS

Recall the times you managed to complete essential tasks amidst the chaos of parenting, focusing on the most critical needs and delegating less-urgent responsibilities.

Consider how you structured your day to accommodate various activities, setting aside dedicated blocks of time for work, family time, self-care and relaxation.

DEVELOPMENT STRATEGIES

Set SMART goals: Define specific, measurable, achievable, relevant and time-bound goals for your business. Break down larger objectives into smaller, actionable steps and allocate time for each task accordingly. Have these lists easily accessible (on paper or electronically) so you can dip in and out of tasks as your time and capacity allows. Without a doubt, so much of my very best work has been done in the front seat of my car, with babes asleep and/or waiting to pick up kids.

Create daily or weekly routines that align with your priorities and goals. Designate specific time slots for work, family time, personal activities and rest, ensuring a balanced and sustainable approach to time management.

ADAPTABILITY IS YOUR STRENGTH

Motherhood is full of surprises, and you have learned to adapt quickly to changing circumstances and environments. Whether it's adjusting your parenting approach to meet the evolving needs of your children or embracing new opportunities as they arise, you approach each situation with flexibility and grace. In business, this same adaptability will enable you to pivot your strategies, innovate in the face of adversity, and stay ahead of the curve in a rapidly changing world.

EXAMPLES OF HIDDEN SKILLS

Recall the times you adjusted your plans on the fly to accommodate unexpected changes or embraced new opportunities that arose unexpectedly.

Consider how you approached parenting with curiosity and an open heart, embracing different perspectives and adapting your approach based on new information or experiences. For me, this is the heart of the parenting journey, right? Once we nail this mindset, it all becomes a lot easier as the expectations and weight of standards fall away.

DEVELOPMENT STRATEGIES

Cultivate a growth mindset, viewing change as an opportunity for learning and growth rather than a threat. Embrace uncertainty, explore new possibilities and remain open to adapting your strategies as needed.

Solicit input from trusted mentors, colleagues or peers on your business ideas, strategies and decisions. Use their insights to refine your plans and adapt to changing circumstances with confidence.

COMMUNICATION IS YOUR POWER

As a mother, you are a master communicator, adept at conveying your thoughts, feelings and expectations with clarity and compassion – sometimes more forcefully than others! You know how to listen deeply, express yourself authentically and foster meaningful connections with those around you. In business, effective communication is the cornerstone of success, enabling you to build rapport with your customers, inspire trust in your employees and lead with integrity and empathy.

EXAMPLES OF HIDDEN SKILLS

Reflect on the times you truly listened to your children, validating their feelings, and demonstrating empathy and understanding.

Consider how you advocated for your children's needs, set boundaries and communicated your expectations with clarity and confidence.

DEVELOPMENT STRATEGIES

Approach interactions with customers, employees and stakeholders with empathy and compassion. Listen actively, validate their feelings and communicate with authenticity and sincerity.

Invest in developing your public speaking and presentation skills to effectively convey your ideas, inspire confidence and engage your audience.

So, my dear entrepreneurial mother, remember this: *You are enough, just as you are.*

You possess within you the skills, the resilience and the determination to build a successful and profitable business; one that not only fulfils your dreams but also creates a meaningful and sustainable impact in the world.

Yes, there will be challenges along the way; that is an inevitable part of the entrepreneurial game. There will be moments of doubt, moments of fear, moments when you feel like giving up. But in those moments, remember the strength that lies within you. Remember the resilience that has carried you through the trials of motherhood. Remember the resourcefulness, the creativity and the adaptability that have been your constant companions on your motherhood journey. Tap into the energy that fuels your fire as a mother and transfer this to entrepreneurship.

In my opinion, if you have grown and birthed a human being (and possibly guided them through their early years of life and beyond), you can do absolutely anything you want and desire. Do not let the world tell you otherwise.

And remember, above all else, that you are not alone. There is a community of entrepreneurial mothers just like you, standing beside you, cheering you on and offering their support and encouragement every step of the way – often in the deepest and darkest hours of night. Reach out to them, lean on them and draw strength from their wisdom and experience, in spirit and in real life.

Together, we will break down the barriers that stand in our way. Together, we will defy the myth of the entrepreneurial unicorn and create a more inclusive and equitable entrepreneurial ecosystem, one where every mother has the opportunity to pursue her dreams, unleash her potential and build a better future for herself, her family, and her community. I know this is your purpose and passion. Anchor back into this over and over again and you will never fail.

With love and solidarity,

Sascha II Fellow Entrepreneurial Mum

Dr Sascha Kowalenko

D r Sascha Kowalenko is a doctor of clinical psychology with over twenty-three years experience, practicing across Australia and internationally in large organisations (public, private and corporate) whilst maintaining a commitment to one-to-one therapeutic practice with women, children and families always. Sascha is passionately driven to impact generational change by leading women to harness the power of their mind, body and spirit so that they can maximise their impact in family, life, career and business.

Sascha established her business, The Silver Lining Collective, when on maternity leave following the birth of her fourth bubba in 2019 and has since grown it to multi-six-figure success. Working one-to-one with many many women and their families and her own lived experience of womanhood, motherhood and life, Sascha has unique insight into the vision, values and vulnerabilities of women driven to have impact in both how they grow up their kids and nurture other relationships whilst also growing career and business aspirations.

Driven by a deep sense of purpose in ensuring that high-achieving women feel less alone, less guilt, overwhelm and defeat the beast that is imposter syndrome, Dr Sascha pivoted her business and is now focused on leading like-minded and -spirited women (entrepreneurs, founders, leaders and CEOs) via courses, group and one-to-one coaching and luxe retreats framed around her ground-breaking methodologies – Mind Design, the POWER Method and the BRAVE Path.

Sascha has a particularly unique skill set of understanding the inner workings of individuals' brains and minds (particularly those in high-pressure and high-performance environments) and the inner (and outer) workings of organisations growing rapidly through startup to scaling. So she is also skilled in supporting leaders and organisations in navigating growth and change from an organisational and clinical psychology and business perspective through her business consulting services.

Learn more about Dr Sascha at drsascha.com.au

THEY TOLD ME I COULDN'T

Shayla Knipe

'You're a mother ... you don't get to have a life, a career, let alone to dream and have aspirations,' he would say as he told me I wasn't worthy of dreaming big, that my dreams were unachievable.

Is this something you would tell your children?

I didn't realise I was in an abusive relationship until I got out, and getting out was the hardest thing I had ever done; separated from everything I'd ever known. Being apart from my daughter was what kept me up at night, what tore me apart and broke my heart daily.

I always knew I could get off my butt and make money, but no-one could help me put my heart back together.

It was at that moment I remembered a quote from Maya Angelou – 'You may not control all the events that happen to you, but you can decide not to be reduced by them.'

In the months, even years, following the break-up, I suppose you could say I was functioning. With low self-esteem and low finances, I got myself back on my feet, starting from scratch. I struggled to be there for my daughter with the mental abuse still being thrown at me. I didn't have the strength within me to fight him. He had the upper hand in everything, telling me I wasn't worthy of having my daughter, punishing me for leaving him and using her against me. I didn't want her to see us fighting any more, I thought I was doing the right thing, keeping the peace, but he had the power because he still had control over me, as he had my little girl. He made all the decisions as he knew how broken I was.

The lack of support and hurdles I had to overcome meant I had to experience my lowest moments. However, I knew I could dwell on what had happened or focus on the future. The dream burning inside me was to create something for my daughter, for us to have a better life together. Every day I would tell myself, *My time will come, my days will get better.*

Life is full of ups and downs. Everyone has their story and their own path through life. It's important to remember this and acknowledge when you're having a down moment, telling yourself tomorrow will be better. But it's just as important to acknowledge the ups and reward yourself for those great moments, as we do all tend to focus on the negatives more than the highlights

Even at a young age, I was a hard worker. I was told many times that I would one day be a boss or a manager as I had a *go-getter* personality. I was the young lady who would step in and take charge of any situation with success and insight.

After the birth of my first daughter, I was nineteen when I started my first business. I was passionate about the pet care industry, having graduated high school as a veterinary nurse, and I started to learn about pet styling, travelling interstate to learn everything I needed to know about the industry.

I wanted to be an innovator, lifting the standard and bringing style to my country town, showing my clients I could offer more than a country shave down. Within twelve months, my small home-based business, which I'd started in my garage, grew into a commercial space. Being young and naive, I didn't understand shop size requirements, fit outs, finances, accounting or taxes. I was as green as you could get, but I had the passion and the focus to make it work. Even though I had a great little business, with thousands of clients and money coming in, I struggled day in and day out to manage and run the business, as I was lacking business education, life experience and the important foundations of running a business, managing money and staff.

My parents never taught me about finances growing up. We didn't have a lot of money and it was never spoken about. Every lesson I've learnt in this life allows me to be a better person and a better parent. I want to ensure I give my children the knowledge they need to be successful in life. I don't just want to give them my hard-earned wealth, I want to give them my wealth of knowledge, so they can continue being successful on this Earth, having the knowledge to be better and do better every day.

When we leave this Earth, do we want our children to carry our wounds or our wisdom?

After four years of struggling with no support, in a toxic relationship and as a young mother, the stress and pressure of running a business, that was growing faster than I could handle, was too much for one person to bear. The weight on my shoulders was just too much. The only option I could see was to walk away, cutting my losses, thinking I would never put myself through that again.

'Businesses don't fail, it's the operations and the managers that fail at business.'

Having nothing else to lose, I found some inner strength and determination for change. At twenty-four years old, I packed whatever would fit in my car and moved to the big city of Melbourne to follow my dream of becoming a travelling member of The Australian Groom Team, hoping I might, one day, represent Australia at the World Dog Grooming Championships, grooming with the world's best. I knew for me to represent Australia, I first had to compete and groom alongside Australia's best. I spent countless hours, long days and even longer nights studying, networking and learning every day.

I would ask myself, Is what I am doing today getting me closer to my goal?

Some days I would answer 'yes' but there were also days of questioning myself at every hurdle.

But I found my space and the level I wanted to play at to achieve the goal I'd set. This was not easy. It was mentally and physically draining, all while managing my emotions day in and day out, not seeing my daughter for months on end, feeling like a complete letdown and a failure as a mother. Winning in the eyes of others was not always positive; I had small-minded people trying to tear me down from all directions. Unfortunately, some people don't want to see you succeed. They tried their hardest to tear me down through bullying on social media – to the point where it divided the entire industry. I learnt who had my back when I needed it most. Those people stepped up and showed up for me; our Pet Industry Association even had my back. This taught me just how strong, powerful, resilient and inspiring I can be for myself and others. At this moment, I discovered who I was deep down and who I needed to be to move forward into my own space.

Melbourne was a life-changing experience I'll never forget. I was lucky to have met some truly inspiring people who I still hold dear to my heart. I added some amazing people to my 'net worth' who I will forever be ready to help if ever they need a helping hand, just as they would for me.

PURPOSE & PASSION

Having some of the best dog groomers and breed experts in the country as my mentors, through this chapter of my life, my determination, drive, passion and purpose led me to pursue this goal for myself and my daughter. After years of dedication, blood, sweat and many tears, I proudly achieved my goal; the dream I was once told was unachievable, that I shouldn't dream so big, that I would be let down if I had such goals. I made the Australian Groom Team. I had made it! I was going international, my tickets were booked and I was packed and ready to go to the world championships … until the world went into total lockdown over a global pandemic, forcing me to pivot once again.

After achieving much success over the years and winning many major awards across Australia, I was given the opportunity to relocate to the beautiful Sunshine Coast in Queensland. I had built a brand for myself, which had presented many amazing opportunities, including presenting live groomings across a variety of royal shows and other city events, to teaching at multiple academies, teaching nationally for large corporate brands, even being asked to compete on a global reality television show known as *Pooch Perfect*, hosted by world-famous actress Rebel Wilson.

Along with stunning beaches and a relaxed atmosphere, living on the Sunshine Coast meant I was close to my family where I had love and support … and of course my daughter. I was able to start visiting her regularly, building an unbreakable bond between us.

The Sunshine Coast became my new home, where I met my soulmate; a man who didn't just love and support my busy go-getter lifestyle and personality, but someone who was willing to ride those waves with me hand in hand, ready to take on the next challenge.

We wanted to buy a house and have children but took the backwards approach. We had children, then started a business. Crazy, right?! We could have put our savings into a home, but instead, we decided to open our first little salon together.

It was a space where I could work and raise our children. I wanted to be a working mother, raising my children and cherishing every moment with them. One quiet Sunday morning, I took my horse out for a ride alone, not realising he had a pinched nerve right under the saddle. As soon as I sat down, I felt his body tense and he threw me off like a rodeo horse. I was no stranger to falling off, growing up riding horses my whole life, however in this instance, I had an unfortunate landing on my coccyx. I felt a crunch and a pop. I didn't think of the worst case, as the adrenaline came in, I thought I would be fine to drive myself to the hospital. Rolling onto my side, slowly getting up to my knees screaming in pain, I slowly and awkwardly walked to my car. The hospital was a forty-minute drive. I called my fiancé telling him what had happened, not realising I had the baby's car seat; he effectively couldn't leave the house. I started driving, not fully understanding the extent of the situation. After ten minutes the adrenaline wore off and my body went into a state of shock from the pain. I pulled over and called for an ambulance. They asked me where the pain was located – I answered, dead set in the middle of my back. It was at that moment I realised something was seriously wrong. When I arrived at the hospital, I was greeted by my frantic fiancé seeing me secured to a stretcher wearing a neck brace, with paramedics advising me to keep still. I still remember the utter feeling of shock and sadness when the doctor walked into the room telling me I had broken my spine. The first thing I thought of was my baby boy and my business. We were six months into owning our business and I had been a full-time working mother with a twelve-month-old little boy at my feet. How was I going to continue? How was I going to care for my family? Would I even be able to walk? How could I handle my business and my clients? I was fully booked out, months in advance! It took a while to comprehend. Little did I realise just how quickly life can be turned upside-down. This is where I learnt to cherish every moment, every smile, every step. We need to stop for a moment each day and see how lucky we are.

We only had twenty-four hours to find day care for my son, as my partner worked full-time, six days a week, and now, because of the injury I'd sustained, I couldn't even care for myself, let alone my baby boy. I couldn't pick him up and give him a cuddle even when he screamed for me. He was too young to understand that it physically wasn't possible for me to hold him. This broke my heart every day. I went home wearing a full-body brace which supported my spine for four months. During this time, my fiancé stepped up, having to care for me and my children.

I was unable to cook, clean, drive, dress my children or even dress myself. I needed him to shower me and help me use the toilet. I could have broken down and given up, *Why me?* But instead, I used this as another life lesson, adding strength, power and determination to get through the other side. I couldn't work *in* my business, so I worked *on* my business. This accident gave me a whole new outlook on my business, as I got to see it from an outside perspective. This led me to start hiring staff, training them to a world-class standard and a higher level of attention to detail. More opportunities came my way, and we acquired our second salon. We then invested in our company allowing us to launch our pet care range, growing our company portfolio into a seven-figure business. We also bought our first home, all within four years. We now have four beautiful children, over six businesses and my bags are packed, once again, to head to the World Grooming Championships, where I hope to travel with my whole family, sharing these amazing opportunities and experiences, with them by my side.

What's next, you may ask, *for Shayla Knipe?* Well, only time will tell … but I have always had big dreams and been able to achieve the unexpected. I'm still dreaming and achieving, now with my children alongside me.

I want my final message to be for all women, mothers, entrepreneurs, to know that there is no limit. We are stronger than we think and when we put our mind to it, we can turn a dream into reality. Bring your kids along with you for this wild adventure, educate them and inspire them to know that no dream is too big if you're willing to work hard for it.

I have learnt that it's never too late – you can always redefine and reinvent yourself. That's the beauty of life. Your failures do not define you; they are, in fact, lessons that help guide you in every stage of your life. By having determination, working hard and staying focused, you can achieve any goal or dream.

My children are my passion, my purpose and drive for everything I continue to do and achieve in this lifetime.

I believe my purpose is to inspire others to follow their dreams and shoot for the stars, as the only limit is what we believe in ourselves. Do not let people say you cannot have it all, you can … you just have to work for it. You can follow your dream while having a family and raising strong confident children to be the next leaders. Showing my children my resilience, passion and drive is so they can be better humans and continue to create a positive ripple effect with everything they do.

I'm passionate about inspiring others, teaching them they can have a career, family and lifestyle; how they can utilise their time better, while maintaining a happy family. We all have the same twenty-four hours in a day … it's all about how we use it. Creating a perfect balanced lifestyle, there is no limit to what we, as women, can accomplish.

Shayla Knipe

Shayla Knipe is the founder and CEO of a seven-figure pet care business, travelling the world inspiring and mentoring pet stylists, business owners and parents about management, leadership and productivity within business and family lifestyle.

As a mother of four, Shayla has taught and inspired hundreds of students globally to become world leading pet stylists and entrepreneurs. Ms Knipe has founded and managed over fifteen businesses across the country and now teaches others how to be better in business, productivity and pet grooming, all while raising her own family.

She is one of Australia's most decorated pet stylists winning many Royal Best in Shows, Australian championships and is a current member of the Australian Groom Team, ready to represent our country at the World Dog Grooming Championships in Belgium.

A few of Shayla's career achievements include: World Grooming Representative for Australia at the European World Grooming Championships; Finalist on a Global reality TV show *Pooch Perfect Australia* hosted by celebrity Rebel Wilson; Multiple Best in Shows, state championships and Australian championships within the dog grooming sector; Empire awards; AusMumpreneur finalist, and many more.

Igniting Your Potential

A Journey of Unexpected Realisations and Growth

Sinead Brace

Do you feel that you are bigger, smarter, bolder and braver, having so much more to offer the world and your career than where you are *right now?* There is a fire within each of us waiting to be ignited; a potential waiting to be unleashed. As Nelson Mandela wisely said, 'There is no passion to be found playing small – in settling for a life that is less than the one you are capable of living.' If you have ever doubted your own potential, if you have ever felt lost in the maze of life, in the chaos of kids and family, living in someone else's shadow, unsure of your own direction and purpose, then this chapter is for you. I am here to reassure you that you can do BIG things. You just need to trust in yourself and remember you are your own biggest advocate.

I always felt I was destined for bigger things, and that one day everything would fall into place. I had dreams of grandeur, from working in an art auction house, having my own yoga studio or owning an art gallery. Yet, nothing compares to the fulfilment I have found in where I stand today. The best part? I carved this path myself. I placed every single brick and paver, and nothing feels better! I'm here today, with not one, but two thriving businesses under my belt, feeling more grounded and fulfilled than ever before.

Join me on a journey of self-discovery and entrepreneurship, where I share my story of overcoming doubts, embracing opportunities and carving my own path to success. The best part is – you can do this too!

EMBRACING MY STORY

Most of my life I've been easily sidetracked by shiny things. Getting caught up in the latest idea, interest or craze, and feeling like maybe this is me, *THIS* is going to be the job, career or hobby that will change my life forever. Then, only to find that the pattern continues, and I never finish what I started!

Sound familiar?

This has been me my whole life.

In school, I was determined to be an art teacher, so straight out of high school, I started studying a bachelor of fine art at university. During my studies, I found a passion for art history and writing, so became obsessed with becoming a curator. I secured an internship in London and was going to do my master's, but instead I moved from Queensland to Western Australia and started working at Coca-Cola. My manager used to love this; *How could an art history major end up selling Coca-Cola?!* But this was me, I became distracted by the new and exciting opportunities that came up in my life. Never seeing anything through to completion or result, no matter how big the opportunity was.

While I was working at Coca-Cola, I was lucky enough to be positioned in regional Western Australia in a mining town called Karratha. This was like heaven for a young couple, filled with boating, bars, travel and the beautiful Australian outback landscapes. During my two years there, I began studying fitness and yoga. Yes, another whirlwind change of direction, but it was what I loved most in this world. Yoga made my soul sing in a quiet town where there wasn't much happening. While I never finished my yoga qualification, I did successfully finish my certificate in group fitness.

Fast-forward a few years and two babies later, back living in Perth, I decided it was time for a job with less travel and time on the road. This is when I started working in an office as a sales coordinator. This enmeshed my sales knowledge and customer service skills with a whole new skill set including CRM management. This role really shaped me for what I do today, and I am so grateful for what I learned during this time. Did I know this at the time? *Of course not!*

Now I bet you are wondering how on earth all of this is relevant – well, let me tell you.

I have learned that people come and go in your life for a reason; they teach you things. This is the same for all the interests, hobbies and jobs you have; you learn so much information across so many different fields that one day, this becomes relevant at the most unexpected time. When you least expect it, you will be using a little piece of information from your past experiences to help bring a project, client's work or a new business to life! It will feel natural and seamless.

HOW IT STARTED

I currently own two businesses; the first is a civil construction/earthmoving business which I support my husband to run, but seemingly, this is his baby. He operates the machine, organises the work, and I support him behind the scenes. We started this business together after moving to Queensland from Perth at the end of 2020. This has now been our family's main source of income since 2021, despite hitting a few curveballs along the way.

Anyone in south-east Queensland in 2021/2 will tell you we had a horrible year of weather. We were hit with La Niña, and it rained like no tomorrow. A great time to start a construction business, right? When you own a business that relies on dry weather … this was killing us, to say it lightly. The financial and mental stresses were making us question our choices and the long-term future of our family's income was seeming uncertain. I had to make the decision between going back to work full-time or really ramping up my own business. You guessed it, naturally I put my big girl pants on and started ramping things up.

At the time I was working in my very small virtual assistant business with my first client, and I was not set up for success. I didn't even know what my job role was called at the time! So, me being me, feeling that ripple of an idea and a challenge in my bones, I decided to choose the road less travelled and started the journey to grow my business. When I say grow, I don't mean just add a client or two – I went hard! I downloaded every template, enrolled for masterclasses, purchased contracts, posted in Facebook groups, spammed people I knew … you name it, I tried it all, hoping that somewhere along the way, it was going to stick and fall into place.

In a matter of a few months, I became fully booked, working with a variety of clients, and was able to substantially increase my hourly rate! This wasn't exactly my dream role. My clients were diverse, and I was doing a lot of subcontractor work, but it was mine.

A bonus: the most rewarding aspect since creating my business is that my income surpasses a traditional full-time wage, every single week!

WHAT IS YOUR LEVEL OF SELF-BELIEF?

When I had the idea to make my business successful and expand, I became more driven than I ever had been before! I had the idea planned out in my head and was ready to run with it. But I was given so many doubts and obstacles by people around me, including some of my nearest loved ones. If I'm honest, the fact that they doubted me kind of pushed me more, made me feel stronger, more determined, and on the first week I earned more than my old full-time wage, I couldn't have been prouder of myself (I did want to rub it in … just a little bit).

The fact that I believed in myself drove my determination. The old Sinead would have listened to everyone else's opinions above my own, and I would have dwelled on people's comments, let them fuel my decisions and fester in the self-doubt, but this time, I was sure. My desire to make something of myself, that is wholeheartedly mine and run with an idea that I truly believed in, led me to where I am today.

THE POWER OF PIVOTING

As my business started to expand, I still wasn't clear on who my ideal client was. The idea of niching down or having a clear client profile seemed far too limiting. I was running with everything that came my way, and let's face it, I wasn't going to turn down the work. I was a woman on a mission.

If I'm honest, sometimes it felt like I was completely winging it and had no idea if what I was pulling together was going to stick. But then I learnt a word that fits me so well; I learnt to *pivot!* This is one of my greatest pieces of advice in business – become comfortable with pivoting. If you view your business as being rigid, unable to flow and move in the directions that it naturally needs to go in, then you will always be limited by your ability to grow and move with what your clients and market needs … and most importantly, what you need!

Let me ask you this.

What valuable opportunities might slip through your grasp in your career if you perceive your business as inflexible, lacking room for change and expansion?

In the beginning, I was offering virtual assistant services, working with all who approached me. This saw me working with executive coaches, athletes, health food companies, subcontracting companies, artists and more. I was offering services in sales, administration, marketing, website development, data entry and account management. It wasn't sustainable, and it didn't fill my cup, but it gave me the opportunity to see what I enjoyed and who I enjoyed working with.

I have pivoted my business from working with a diverse client base to now offering a bespoke service to my high-value clients. Just like my business, every person I support has a unique offer and skill set themselves.

Pivoting has been vital for my business, allowing growth, higher rates and improved services. Now, offering bespoke executive-level support, I connect with clients whose values align with mine and support their business confidently. I choose my clients not solely based on the support they are looking for, but more about their character, vision and direction for their business.

NAVIGATING BEING A PARENT AND THE BUSINESS WORLD

'I think every working mom probably feels the same thing: You go through big chunks of time where you're just thinking, *This is impossible – oh, this is impossible.* And then you just keep going and keep going, and you sort of do the impossible.' – Tina Fey

Corkscrew Creative was born with the *WHY* of being there for my kids. A bit cliché, but that was all I wanted. I had the idea when I first became pregnant of being a stay-at-home parent and spending the days cooking and crafting with my kids. I soon learned this was not a reality, and it also takes a certain type of person to be able to do this without wanting and needing more for themselves beyond being a mother. Returning to work when both of my kids were around six months old, I experienced the pressure of balancing my role as a mother and wife, meeting my employer's expectations, managing work hours and striving for personal success.

As time went on, COVID-19 hit, jobs changed, and we moved interstate, I found myself back in this state of not wanting to go back to work full-time and our old lifestyle. I couldn't do it. It wasn't really about leaving my kids; it was more about having to do it all. The mental and physical load of being a mother. The school-day routines, the housework, the washing, the cooking, the dishes, the homework, and then let's add in a sneaky nine-to-five job somewhere. It felt like it was impossible.

I knew from previous jobs how this added stress on myself and my relationships, and I didn't want this a second time around. So, when I was working on my WHY, it became about being there for my kids, but also being there for myself. Allowing myself the necessary space and time to navigate life in the directions I desire and granting myself space when it's needed.

I wanted to demonstrate to my kids that mothers can do great things too; we really do the impossible every day! Mothers can make life and business fall hand in hand and rock it!

Mothers once were able to rely on their village to support them, but now, it is more common that she is her own village. I want my kids to see that you can juggle it all, even if the balls do drop sometimes. Over the years, I hope to demonstrate to them that they can push societal expectations regarding their careers, and that they can achieve their goals, even if it means taking a challenging or unconventional path.

PURPOSE

I don't want to fool you for a moment, or for you to think I set out on this journey to fulfil my purpose, knowing exactly what it looks like. That is far from the truth.

When I started out, as you've read, there was no clear indication of where I was going, just a longing to achieve; to make something of myself, earn some money to contribute to my family and maybe push a few societal boundaries along the way. It wasn't until I listened to one of my beautiful clients Sheila Vijeyarasa's new podcasts that I had a moment where I went, *HOLY SH*T! I'm doing exactly what I've been preparing to do my whole life, and oh my gosh … it feels good!*

While I will continue to pivot and continue to grow, I know my purpose is still being developed. My short-term purpose is leading me to my longer-term purpose, and I am so grateful to her podcast for providing me with this knowledge, along with the ability to feel a sense of calm and motivation in what I am doing and achieving every day.

CONTINUED GROWTH

If I could offer any advice to those considering their entrepreneurial journey, especially in the realm of support services, it would be this: defy the limitations others place upon you. Grasp every opportunity that becomes available and embrace the power of pivoting.

You've witnessed my journey unfold, observed as my skills evolved and my business transformed. From a virtual assistant, to now removing the labels to offer a bespoke executive-level service that fills my cup every day, to whatever the future holds next. I am fortunate to support exceptionally gifted individuals – artists, authors, fitness professionals, television figures and coaches – who reintegrate all my past experiences and interests into my present reality. What once seemed like unrelated studies and hobbies, now enhance the support I provide in my business daily.

But my business journey is far from over. As I continue to delve deeper into self-discovery, learning from both my experiences and my clients, I am driven forward by the endless possibilities that lie ahead. With each new revelation, I am reminded that the only limit to my growth is the sky itself, and I eagerly anticipate the next chapter in the evolution of Corkscrew Creative.

How will your story unfold?

Sinead Brace

As a mother to Kiara and Eli, two fur babies Alby and Rusty and a supportive wife to my husband William, my journey into starting my own business took me by surprise. We had recently started the family earthmoving business Elite Trim, and I wasn't expecting to embark on my own journey into entrepreneurship so soon, but life frequently takes us down unexpected paths. I believe that all of life's twists and turns have each contributed to my purpose and readiness to start my business, Corkscrew Creative.

From a young age, I felt a calling to pursue something beyond the ordinary. Although my original dreams revolved around art and becoming a curator, life's plans led me on a diverse and well-travelled path – from working at Coca-Cola as a business development executive throughout Western Australia to embracing the serenity of yoga in the Australian outback to working in sales in New Zealand. Throughout these travels, I have been blessed to learn skills and wisdom from incredibly inspiring individuals, who have all contributed to my success. Each encounter has left a mark, encouraged my journey and strengthened my determination to seize every opportunity.

Despite my varied experiences and interests, my desire to find something I loved kept me driven. Each job role I held, whether in sales, administration or exploring different hobbies, contributed to the skill set that I now could not live without. However, it was not until I was confronted with the challenge of balancing motherhood with a traditional career that I recognised the importance of paving my own path.

Harnessing my desire to be present for my family while pursuing my personal goals, I took a leap of faith and started Corkscrew Creative. While it began with me hosting mindfulness art classes, which drew on my bachelor of fine art and my love of yoga and meditation, it has now grown into something far more fulfilling and diverse. Corkscrew Creative offers bespoke business support to startup businesses and entrepreneurs. This journey was not without its setbacks, obstacles and pivoting, but understanding my purpose and believing in myself supported me in transforming my new business into a thriving venture.

Growing up amongst the hustle and bustle of Gold Coast suburbs, my childhood seems worlds away from the rural lifestyle that my family and I now live. My children are blessed with a country life, something that I wish all those years ago I let my mum provide for me. My mum is strong and independent and was always dedicated to providing me the best life possible, despite my teenage rebellions and the obstacles that life threw her way. This taught me the value of perseverance, independence and having the courage to grow amidst adversity – a foundation I carry with me every day.

Today, as the owner of Corkscrew Creative, I am guided by a sense of purpose and a vision for the future. I am eager to continue exploring new ideas, growing my business and inspiring others to recognise their own potential. With each obstacle I face, I view it as an opportunity for growth and transformation, confident in my ability to overcome and thrive.

corkscrewcreative.com.au

Finding Yourself Through the Stars

Sophia Pallas

I don't know what I'm supposed to do now.

I was sitting in the supermarket car park, like I'd done many times before, sending a voice message to a friend.

I thought I knew where my life was going, and now I'm just floating.

It was 2019, and I'd just discovered my marriage of eight years was over. While the heartbreak, betrayal and pure shock were overwhelming, the thing that struck me most about that time was how completely I'd lost touch with myself.

I'd either forgotten, or never really understood, who I was and what I wanted.

The thing is, I couldn't blame the relationship, or motherhood, or put it down to any one thing in particular. I'd simply allowed myself to get lost along the way through my external identities. I was a wife, then a mother and then I threw myself into my copywriting business when my kids were tiny.

There were fragments of who I was, but nothing solid enough to hold onto at that destabilising time. And my personal and business life seemed to be crumbling because I felt like nothing fit me anymore.

'Maybe you should talk to Kat,' my friend said. 'She's an astrologer and she always helps me get clarity when I'm struggling with something.'

At the time, I was deeply sceptical that *anything* could help me find my way.

I'd tried all sorts of things to figure out what I wanted to do or where my passion was – personality tests, strength assessments, dozens of self-help books and countless online trainings.

Nothing seemed to work for me.

Yet, I was desperate for answers. Something kept telling me there was a missing piece of the puzzle I needed to find – an insight into myself, and why all this was happening. And so, a few weeks later, I found myself on a grainy Skype call with Kat, the Shamanic astrologer, as she tried to show me my astrology chart (what looked like a circle with loads of lines through it) via my phone screen.

I didn't know it then, but that day changed my life.

Kat said things about me I'd never heard before and yet felt deeply true. She told me about my personality, my values and my quirks – much more than I had known about myself and my Capricorn Sun sign. It was as if she could see the things I'd always known about myself but I'd been too afraid to express. I was finally being noticed and validated, not just my strengths, but my unique challenges too. There was no going back once I knew those things, and when the call ended, I wanted more. I had to find out how astrology worked, so I could unravel and understand more about myself and the people around me.

I had to go deeper.

Thanks in part to a very different world in 2020 and 2021, I became consumed with learning as much as I could about astrology. I binged every astrology podcast I could find. I bought books and enrolled in course after course, to go deeper and learn more. I invested in readings with different astrologers to make sure what Kat had told me wasn't just by accident – it wasn't. And surprisingly, that circle with all the lines and numbers on it started to make sense to me.

It was like a light had been turned on in my mind. I became fascinated with the geometry, the symbols and the mythology of astrology. I was almost 'remembering' astrology rather than learning it for the first time. And I realised what I was learning about myself and my purpose, my style and my way of being would be so powerful for my clients to know about themselves as well.

But there was also fear. Could I really talk about this to clients? Was this really possible? I remember telling my business coach about it at the time, nervously thinking, *What if she says this will never work?* Instead, she told me: 'Of course, this makes total sense for you. It's like the missing piece you've been looking for.' She was right.

I started to bring astrology into my copywriting and coaching sessions with clients and they loved it, even the clients I thought would be hesitant, like marketers, lawyers and psychologists.

I realised the reason astrology is so powerful for business is because many entrepreneurs don't have the self-awareness they need to fulfil their potential.

They haven't fully identified their zone of genius and their specific gaps.

Once you know your birth chart and can start to understand yourself in this way, you're able to feel authentic and excited about your business again. You also free yourself from imposter syndrome and that debilitating feeling of being a copy of someone else.

Soon my brain adapted, and I saw the benefits of using astrology everywhere. I used it to plan my schedule and client projects. I used it for my clients' program launches, to add personality to lack-lustre copy and even for my online dating approach!

But pivoting from traditional marketing and copywriting into this 'woo-woo' realm of astrology for business wasn't easy. Turns out, once you've found your purpose, living it requires *work*. And not just surface-level, get-the-job-done work – real, deep inner work too.

Here's what I discovered:

- Knowing more about yourself means you need to look at your shadow side too.

There are many benefits to understanding more about yourself and how you naturally operate in business.

A higher level of self-awareness is linked with more confidence and better leadership abilities. But we don't always have the right tools to access it. Or we focus too much on one part of our personality and stay blind to core issues that could be holding us back.

Astrology gives you access to deep self-awareness: what you do, why you do it and even the blocks you need to overcome to do things better.

For example, when you know you have a challenging placement of Mars (the planet of action, energy and assertiveness) in your chart – step back and notice the times you let other people dictate the decisions you make in business.

Maybe you keep finding yourself in situations where you people-please or follow the crowd instead of owning and prioritising your own energy and inner authority. But if you want to grow your business, these kinds of patterns will hold you back from making more powerful decisions and getting stronger results.

Astrology is a symbolic tool that can help you become aware of tendencies like this, so you can adapt and change or put things in place to stop the pattern from continuing.

- Follow the cycles – don't expect every week to be a record-breaker.

Something both astrology and entrepreneurship teach us is to allow for cycles of growth and contraction. Not every week can be a record-breaker, nor should it be.

There will be loads of highs, but in order to experience those highs, we need to allow times of rest, reflection and retreat. These are the natural cycles of life, but we often get so swept up in 'winning' at business that we forget.

Looking to the Moon can be a fantastic way to get back in touch with this natural cycle. That's why I encourage my clients to work with the phases of the Moon when planning their promotions throughout the year.

If you follow the cycles of the moon in your business, just like many experienced gardeners do – you'll learn that the times when the Moon is invisible (or brand new) can be the most fertile. This is the time to plant new seeds that will grow over the next phases of the Moon's cycle – eventually bringing the harvest you desire. It's in this quiet phase where you can reflect, plan and set intentions for your business, setting up the growth cycle ahead.

And it's often in these times of pause that the magic happens. Maybe you discover a new idea for a course or a product. Or maybe you connect with someone who brings five referrals to you down the line.

Don't buy into the hype that your business can be a twenty-four-seven harvest. It's not possible. There have to be times for planning, planting and germination.

• Some people won't get it, and that's okay.

When I first pivoted my business to incorporate astrology, I lost a lot of email subscribers.

It was to be expected, I suppose.

They came to me for copywriting tips and now here I was talking about the phases of the Moon and the transits of Jupiter … It was all a bit too much for some people. And that's totally okay.

In business, we need to accept we're not going to vibe with everyone. Maybe even as you're reading this you're thinking, *Astrology and business – that's madness!* I get it, I really do. I was just like you a few years ago – until I discovered the practical benefits of working with astrology. The key is not to let other people's opinions or approval influence your decision to give your business your all.

If you give up because you get a few unsubscribes or lose some social media followers, you're not serving your purpose or following your passion. Don't allow yourself to be derailed by someone who's never going to be an ideal client, instead acknowledge all the people out there who want what you have to offer.

You're also not being true to who you are and what you value. You're allowing others to decide what's worthy, instead of being guided by your inner truth.

Astrology has become something that connects me back to my inner compass. My own truth.

Whenever I feel wobbly about something I'm putting out into the world, or if I get a negative comment on social media, I remind myself of what I value and what I'm here to contribute to the world. These days, I actually enjoy unsubscribes, because it tells me the people who remain on my email list really want to be there. And that feels super satisfying.

- Find ways to complement your strengths and adjust for your weaknesses.

The beauty of knowing your strengths through astrology is that you also know how you can complement these and adjust for your weaknesses.

If, for instance, you have a lot of 'fire' energy in your chart but little to no 'earth', it's a great idea to consider how you can incorporate more earth support into your business.

Fire energy is all about ideas, inspiration and charisma, while earth energy is grounding and practical. A fire-dominant entrepreneur probably needs some extra support with the structural and even technical aspects of their business. Meanwhile, an earth-dominant entrepreneur might need support finding ways to gain inspiration and build their presence and visibility.

Understanding these astrological energies can help you plan your business approach, best marketing strategies and the way you interact with clients and team members.

For instance, an entrepreneur with a lot of water energy might do well in businesses that require empathy and emotional connection. They can use their natural ability to understand what others need to provide top-notch service.

On the other hand, an entrepreneur with a lot of air energy might excel in business roles that need fast thinking and good communication – like consulting or public relations.

By being more aware of how these different energies play out in your business approach, you can create a more balanced and efficient dynamic. This not only uses your natural strengths to your advantage but also adjusts for any weaknesses, leading to a more successful and enjoyable business.

- Having people around who support your mission and understand your purpose is invaluable.

The people who 'get it' and love what you do will continue to inspire you to do more and do better.

Keep these people around and lean on them when you feel wobbly. Their support is absolutely invaluable to your success. It might only be a handful of people to start with, but the more passion you show for what you do, the more people will be naturally attracted to it and want to support it.

I couldn't have transformed my business without the help of business friends and clients who spread the word about what I do. Not to mention that getting encouragement from people who share my vision has created an environment where fresh and exciting ideas can form.

I've realised this collection of friends, clients and colleagues isn't just there to cheer me on – they're vital partners. They provide feedback, challenge my ideas, and help me step out of my comfort zone (which I absolutely need as a Taurus rising who loves being comfortable!).

Plus, as your network grows, it becomes a rich resource for collaboration and new opportunities, speeding up your business growth. In fact, my network is one of the key reasons I started a podcast. I wanted to be able to share my business astrology insights with more people and collaborate with other online business owners and astrologers to spread the word.

Ultimately, the strength of your network can significantly influence your business' path. I've learned that when I take care of my relationships, interact genuinely and always look to bring value to those around me – my business blooms. It not only survives challenges but thrives in a supportive community that shares my vision.

THE UPSHOT OF ALL THIS?

With the help of astrology, so many amazing things have changed and unfolded for me since I uncovered more about myself and my purpose. My business has evolved and turned into something I'm truly excited about. I navigated some big personal growth, and I met an incredible partner.

But it all came down to embracing my authentic self. Not just the nice, comfortable parts, but also my unique challenges.

I believe the deep self-awareness I've found through astrology has fuelled my confidence and leadership abilities in life and business. It's helped me make decisions that truly resonate with who I am.

What I know for sure is that it's an ongoing process to completely understand yourself and your work in the world. But when you're invested in knowing who you are, what you value and what you're here to contribute – it will always bring you back on track.

I still have long voice message chats in the supermarket car park, but I also know I have all the answers within me.

Sophia Pallas

S ophia Pallas is an astrologer, copywriter and online business strategist. She's also the host of the award-winning podcast *Cosmic Business Breakthrough*.

After spending more than fifteen years working with big brands and entrepreneurs to improve their copy and marketing with mainstream strategies – she's flipped the script.

Now, Sophia uses the ancient wisdom of astrology to help online entrepreneurs dig deep, understand themselves and crystalise their message for more growth and satisfaction in business.

Her clients love working with her to craft copy and marketing strategies that vibe with their values, speak to their dream customers, and fit their lifestyle and natural energy cycles.

Perpetually curious about the 'big' questions, Sophia started exploring astrology at a young age but her Capricornian scepticism got in the way.

It wasn't until her life and business 'imploded' in 2019 that she was drawn back in and forever changed by what she discovered about herself through astrology.

Sophia lives on the Gold Coast with her three children and her husband – who she met after changing her online dating approach thanks to understanding her astrology chart.

She was awarded bronze in both the Marketing Services and Podcast of the Year categories at the 2023 AusMumpreneur Awards.

For more, visit sophiapallas.com or follow @sophiapallas on Instagram.

Take the Leap

Victoria Howe

Sitting on a plane thousands of feet in the air, watching my six-month-old asleep in the cot in front of me, I took my husband's hand; we squeezed tight, but said nothing. We had just left our entire lives behind, our friends, our family, our jobs – *everything* – to move to the other side of the world to embark on an adventure.

Sure, my husband had a job, but we had never previously stepped foot in WA, Australia. What were we thinking?

I had taken the leap. I took the opportunity in front of me. I thought, *What a fantastic adventure, what a life we are going to have. If it doesn't work out, we can go back, can't we?* What stories would I be able to tell, what memories would I make. I was happy. I was excited to take the leap.

Our journey through life is unknown, but I believe we are given opportunities to frame our life, chances to make decisions that determine the next course of events. Of course, we have all missed opportunities or made wrong decisions, but we can always steer back on the right track. Taking the leap to me is like a fork in the road; choose right and take that leap or choose left, stay safe and maybe miss an opportunity.

Taking the leap doesn't mean doing something with no thought or planning, though, it means to take the chance offered to you with calculated risk. Does it fit in with your goals and dreams, your morals and your values? Are we certain it won't cause anyone harm? Will it bring you happiness? What is your gut telling you? If you are ticking those boxes, then what are you waiting for?

Taking the leap has shown me the strength I have. To be able to raise a family with no help. To move to a town where I know *absolutely no-one*. To do things I have never done before. Making yourself vulnerable will show you your strengths and your weaknesses, both of which are fantastic learning tools.

'I want to wake up tomorrow smarter than I did today.'

We have a choice to learn from every situation, take it or leave it, the choice is yours.

BE HAPPY

What are we doing this all for? Why are you reading this book? Why am I writing this chapter?

It makes me happy, that's why.

Although I will be the first to admit, I do many things that don't make me happy – laundry, small talk, paying bills. This is not the happiness I am talking about; I'm talking about your life, your soul. Are you happy?

Is it too early for me to say, *If you're not happy, change it?* It's not that easy, some would say. However, I believe it is. It comes back to choice; you can either choose to stay or choose to be happy.

Happiness, for me, is the key to it all. So, I make it a priority to ensure my happiness. Yes, this could be seen as selfish, but I tell you what, things run smoother when I'm happy. I'm more efficient, more organised, I can go to sleep at night and wake up in the morning, I'm fitter and healthier, only having one glass of wine, not two. My relationships run smoother; the kids don't get shouted at. When I'm happy, I can communicate my needs, both in business and personally.

Here are a few things I like to do to ensure that, the majority of the time, I am happy.

SURROUND YOURSELF WITH GOOD PEOPLE

Like-minded people, kind people, people that celebrate your success or achievement. A little tip, look at someone's face when you share good news. They may say they are happy for you, but they can't hide their facial expressions. Do their eyes light up, their cheeks lift? Do they smile? Then, that, my friends, is someone who really cares – if not, buyer beware.

Don't be friends with the 'cool' kids because of status and popularity. Seek out those people who are kind, helpful, smart. Find people who champion you and your business, even if they have no idea what you do. You don't need to drop people that don't fit those criteria, but you can limit your time with them. I guarantee, when you start spending time with runners, before you know it, you'll be running your first race and thinking, *How did I get here?* The same goes for business owners and leaders.

'All that glitters is not gold.' – William Shakespeare

If you find yourself disliking someone, question – are you jealous? If you are jealous of someone, ask yourself why? Then ask yourself, *Has that person done anything wrong to me?* No? Then perhaps you might be able to learn from that person. Find out how they have achieved or are doing the things you want to do. Turn the tables on your thinking.

There are two rules in the Dojo: 1) You don't hit anyone. 2) Don't let anyone hit you.

Now, they are talking in the physical sense, yes, but use that philosophy throughout life: don't be unkind to others and don't let them be unkind to you.

HOBBIES

Get a hobby. What is it you really like to do? Go do it! Allocate time during your week to do something you really like. Yes, there are plenty of other more pressing things to do, but even just one hour a week will bring you joy and happiness. Give yourself a break from it all. What's the point if you can't enjoy the things you love?

WORKOUT

Prioritise being fit and healthy; easy to say, not so easy to do. My husband and I have noticed our mood and productivity increases after we have done some exercise in the morning. Go for a walk, workout, yoga, run – whatever gets you moving. Investing time in yourself is also investing time in your business and your happiness.

GIVE BACK

Ask a busy person, they will always find time. Give your time to help others; join a local charity, volunteer at events, coach a team. Not only will this provide well-needed assistance to a community group, but it's also a fantastic way to network; you never know who you might meet. The pride you feel when you can help others does nothing but fill you with happiness.

LOVE

Love hard and love well. I can't mention happiness without mentioning my family, my loving husband Nick, our 'gentleman' George, our 'princess' Penelope and the 'little one' Tabitha. Your family might not be anything like mine, but whoever it is, whatever it is ... love hard. Sharing and receiving love is so special. Love is shown in friendships too, don't forget that. Definitions of love go from an intense feeling of deep affection to like or enjoy very much. I'm sure you can think of someone who fits that definition … and when you do – love them!

Finally, and some may say most importantly, acknowledge that we are going to have days when we are unhappy. Things just might go wrong. You might get a speeding ticket, you might have a health scare. Its okay to be unhappy for a moment. Embrace that unhappiness and what can you learn from it. Acknowledging a bad situation or bad mood will go a long way to changing that feeling.

SET GOALS

'So, what's your plan?' I asked a friend one day. I could see she was studying and was curious. We had a chat and carried on with our day. A month or so later I was shocked to hear my friend was packing up and leaving town. 'Why?' I asked. She smiled and looked at me saying, 'It's your fault, actually.' She went on to explain that when I had asked her what her plans were, she had none. She had dreams, but no goals or real plans. She realised in that moment she needed to pull her finger out and go chase her dreams. Not because of me, because once she set her goal, she began the process of working hard to achieve it.

Setting goals is so important, not only in life but in business. Do you have a business plan? No? Why not? Hold yourself accountable, set a goal and work damn hard towards that goal.

Don't be afraid to amend your goals. I share goals with my husband, and I have personal ones. Between us, our goals have changed as we've grown. We are now onto goal number three or four; having never thought we would hit goal one, let alone set more.

If you don't have a goal, how do you know what choice to make when an opportunity arises? How do you know if you should turn right or left at the fork in the road?

Here are some ways I set my goals:

Think about what makes you happy, what is going to sustain that happiness, and then write it down. Once on paper, break that goal down and work out how you are going to achieve it. Make smaller goals, all with the aim of getting to the big one.

BE REALISTIC

Being a millionaire in two months is not a realistic goal. Set a goal that is achievable. Some use the SMART anagram which is very useful, but quite simply, set a goal that you know you can achieve with hard work, determination and passion. Remember goals can be weekly, monthly, yearly or even further into the future; planning for retirement is goal-setting.

GOALS SET?

Then start, get a move on. What are you waiting for? We can always find a reason why *not* to start something, but that is your choice. Are you going right or left at the fork in the road?

My goal-setting is both daily and long-term. If you know me you know I love a list; glass boards on the walls, a pad on the kitchen counter and to-do lists on my phone.

My life is that hectic that if I didn't have a list of things I needed to do, I just wouldn't work efficiently. It also helps my mind rest at night, knowing I haven't forgotten to do something,

So, a small goal like mowing the lawn can be achieved today, and a long-term goal of hitting the international market, are worlds apart, but they are both goals. The confidence boost you get from ticking off a goal can't be bought; it is earned and earned only by you. But don't sell yourself short, *give yourself a challenge, and you will grow.*

THE HUSTLE

'Do whatever it takes to achieve your goal.'

I repeat, 'Do whatever it takes to achieve your goal.' If you need work two jobs, clean toilets, sell bras, teach swimming, pack eggs, wait tables, cut cauliflowers … then do it. If you need to attend events to network, then, do it. Do you need to apply for a grant? Then do it! Do you need to ask for help writing a business plan? Then do it!

Did I think achieving goals was going to be easy? Absolutely not. If your goal was easy to achieve, then you did yourself a disservice. Goals are tough, they are hard work. Name me a successful person who said it was easy to get to where they are now. You will have to work every day towards your goal, and I call that *hustling*.

It's no secret that I tried several ideas before I got to where I am now. No shame in it at all. The goal was still the same, it just adapted as ideas were tried and tested. It's okay to adapt to the market, change your course, give up something. Being able to do that is a skill. Some may see it as a failure but it's those people you don't want around. Hang with the people who remind you that every mistake, as well as every success, is a learning opportunity.

I didn't go from a police officer to farmer overnight, the end goal for us as a family stayed the same.

We have discussed taking the leap and the opportunities when they present, now I wonder if you thought those opportunities *just appear*. No, it's the hustle that provides these opportunities. How do you think I got to write in this book? I made the opportunity become a reality by working for it.

Don't know how to do something? Read about it, go on a course, go to a workshop, watch YouTube … but do whatever it takes to achieve your goals. The police woman in me, though, wants to remind you that *whatever* means anything legal.

Know this, all those things I listed in the first paragraph of this section, are things I have done, and some I still do to this day. I still have goals I have not achieved, and I am hustling towards them right now. Once I get them, you're damn right I'm going to set some more.

ENJOY

So now you are set up, you've taken the leap, you are happy, you have set goals and are hustling to achieve them. What now?

Well … enjoy the ride.

Enjoy every moment of the memories you are making, of the legacy you are leaving. Enjoy achieving goals and setting new ones.

Own the choices you've made – good and bad; they make you human. But do make sure you learn from each one of them.

Champion other winners, support leaders, don't get jealous. Be kind, be civil but don't take the hits. Take the path of opportunities and don't be scared to change everything you know; you never know, it might just be the best decision you've ever made.

I know my leap was.

Good luck.

Love, Vic xxx

Victoria Howe

Hi, my name is Victoria Howe, and I am the director and co-owner with my husband of South West Snails. Yes, you read that correctly snails or escargot.

We live with our three children on a forty-acre property in rural South West WA, and our dream of working from the farm in a sustainable business has now become a reality.

So, what do we do and how do we do it? Well, that might take an entire book, but we take the common garden snail and turn it into a high-end restaurant dish, going through processes to clean and purge the snails before sending them live straight to professional kitchens. We work alongside farmers to reduce pests, reduce the chemicals they need to use and turn those pests into profitable produce.

How did we come up with the idea? We found our dream property and now we needed to find a way to use it. So, I googled it. *What to do on my acreage.* Google results: *50 things to do on your farm* number twenty-six was 'snail farming'.

I read and read and researched and thought, *Let's do it, let's give it a go.*

PURPOSE & PASSION

We are now the only snail farm in WA, and one of a handful in Australia. Successfully running our business on our farm with our family.

This, however, is not how I thought my life would end up. Originally from the UK, I had spent time in Australia as a five-year-old and then again at eighteen but yearned to return. To do what, I didn't know.

I joined the police force in 2005 and met my husband at police academy that year, my career as a police officer took me down many exciting paths, but after ten years, getting married and looking to start a family, we wanted a change. The opportunity to apply to the Western Australia Police presented itself and we took the leap. Not realising that opportunity set in motion the next nine years of my life where I have ended up here, in this book talking to you.

Since arriving in Australia, I threw myself into community life and joined what felt like every community group going from Chamber of Commerce president to agricultural show secretary and member of The Lions Club, from board of management to committee for pony club, swim club and hockey club, along with being an active member of the local bush fire brigade.

Our dream, though, was to humbly work on our farm for ourselves and become financially free, that's it – no thrills, no bells and whistles.

What's come with that dream and the hustle to get there is much more, with radio and TV interviews, award nominations, public speaking, event invitations, newspaper articles and blogs. Representing women in farming and agriculture, new industry and choosing to go right not left. Maybe our goal will change, but for now we have hit the ground running and are loving every minute.

Check us out at southwestsnails.com

THIS BOOK CHANGES LIVES

Proceeds from the sale of this book go to providing marginalised women in business with scholarships to enable them to receive support, mentoring and education through The Women's Business School.

Aligning with the United Nations SDG goals for gender equality, The Women's Business School scholarships are awarded to women in remote and rural areas, First Nations women, migrant women, survivors of domestic violence, women with disability and chronic illness and those facing financial hardship.

We believe that investing in women is the most powerful way to change the world, and these scholarships provide opportunities for deserving women to participate in an incubator program for early stage startups and businesses and an accelerator program for high-potential entrepreneurs ready to scale their companies and expand globally.

You can read more about the work of The Women's Business School Scholarship Program and how they're changing the world here:

thewomensbusinessschool.com/scholarship

ABOUT PEACE & KATY AND SPEAKING OPPORTUNITIES

Peace and Katy are the dynamic duo behind AusMumpreneur, Australia's number-one community for mums in business; The Women's Business School, providing dedicated education for aspiring and established female founders; Women Changing the World Press, amplifying the voices of thought leaders, female founders and women changing the world; and Women Changing the World Investments, providing opportunities for capital for female founders.

Peace Mitchell is a TEDx speaker, international keynote speaker, retreat facilitator and workshop presenter.

If you want your audience to be captivated by a heart-centred, warm and engaging thought leader and speaker then look no further.

With experience delivering keynote presentations on connection, business success, magic and productivity, there's nothing Peace loves more than engaging with your delegates to make your event a huge success.

If you've got an online or in-person event coming up and want to create a magical, warm and engaging atmosphere, please get in touch.

peace@womensbusinesscollective.com
+61 431 615 107

ABOUT THE WOMEN'S BUSINESS SCHOOL

The Women's Business School is a business school designed exclusively for women. Providing opportunities for innovative female founders to scale their startup, connect with fellow founders and gain advice and guidance from successful entrepreneurs and experts. Through the award-winning incubator and accelerator programs, founders receive world-class entrepreneurial education from a team of high-level experts and entrepreneurs as well as mentoring, advice and access to successful female entrepreneurs across a range of industries. If you're ready to take your business to the next level apply today!

thewomensbusinessschool.com

ABOUT AUSMUMPRENEUR

Australia's number-one community for mumpreneurs. The AusMumpreneur Awards are a national event recognising and celebrating Australia's best and brightest mums in business. Held annually, these awards recognise the incredible women who are balancing business and motherhood and creating innovative, high-quality and remarkable brands across a range of industries.

ausmumpreneur.com

ABOUT WOMEN CHANGING THE WORLD PRESS

Women Changing the World Press publishes thought leaders, female founders and women who are committed to making the world a better place through their words and actions. We believe that investing in women is the most powerful way to change the world and we are passionate about amplifying women's voices, stories and ideas and providing more opportunities for women to share their message with the world. If you have a story that the world needs to hear get in touch today.

wcwpress.com

ABOUT WOMEN CHANGING THE WORLD AWARDS

The Women Changing the World Awards recognises, acknowledges and celebrates the trailblazers, changemakers and visionary action-takers. Providing a platform to amplify the achievements, accomplishments and work that women around the world are doing to make a difference in big and small ways. We believe that by elevating women, their ideas and their impact we can create a ripple effect that not only celebrates these women and the incredible work that they do but also inspires others to take action and make the world a better place in their own way too.

wcwawards.com

www.ingramcontent.com/pod-product-compliance
Lightning Source LLC
Chambersburg PA
CBHW030455210326
41597CB00013B/678